89

3000 800013 73709
St. Louis Community College

D1282747

WITHDRAWN

C-1

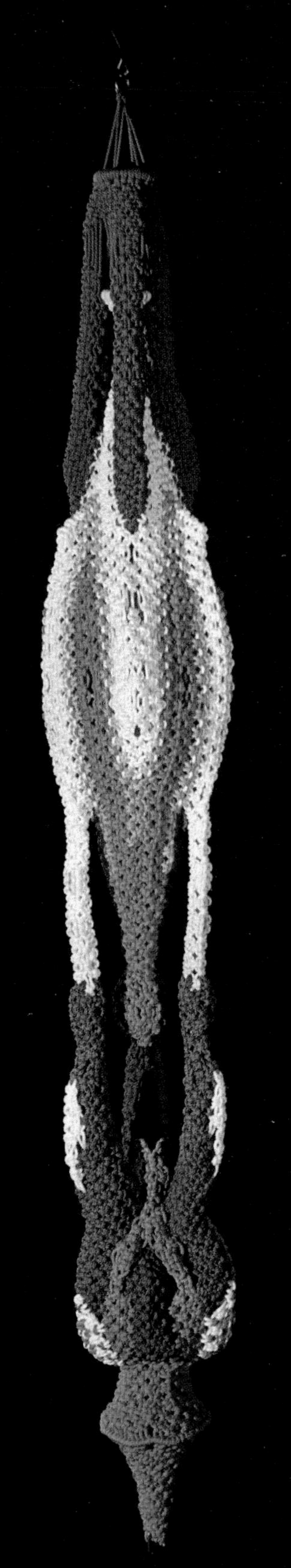

C

C-5

C-3

C-4

C-6

C-7

C-10

C-8

C-11

C-9

FAR BEYOND THE FRINGE

Three-Dimensional Knotting Techniques Using Macrame & Nautical Ropework

Eugene Andes

All articles pictured are the work of Gene & Ellen Andes

VAN NOSTRAND REINHOLD COMPANY
New York Cincinnati Toronto London Melbourne

BOOKS BY EUGENE ANDES

PRACTICAL MACRAME
FAR BEYOND THE FRINGE

Dedicated, with thanks, to Rosa Delia Vasquez

Van Nostrand Reinhold Company Regional Offices:
New York Cincinnati Chicago Millbrae Dallas
Van Nostrand Reinhold Co. International Offices:
London Toronto Melbourne

Library of Congress Catalog Card Number: 72-7845
ISBN: 0 442-20351-9 cloth
ISBN: 0 442-20353-5 paper

Designed by Rosa Delia Vasquez

Black & white photography by Jane Lougee Bryant

Published by Van Nostrand Reinhold Company
450 West 33rd Street, New York, N. Y., 10001
Published simultaneously in Canada by
Van Nostrand Reinhold Limited
16 15 14 13 12 11 10 9 8 7 6 5 4 3 2

Captions for color photos

C-1. Hanging in Macra-Cord. (Photo courtesy of Lily Mills.)

C-2. Hanging in Macra-Cord. Height approximately 40 inches. (Photo courtesy of Lily Mills.)

C-3. Lamp shade—Lily Mills Co. Macra-Cord.

C-4. Lamp—varnished cotton cord.

C-5. Hanging lamp in Macra-Cord.

C-6. Lamp with stained glass panels.

C-7. Macrame vests in nylon seine twine.

C-8. Vest in Lily Mills Co.'s Macra-Cord.

C-9. Wall hanging in cotton seine twine.

C-10. Rope swing in cotton rope and seine twine.

C-11. Cradle: Cotton seine twine and acrylic yarn.

C-12. Hanging lamp in cotton seine twine.

HOW TO USE THIS BOOK AND/OR CONTENTS PAGE

In addition to its obvious uses as a table-leveler or a fire-starter, this book may serve as a guide for the knotter who wishes to make something beyond belts and handbags. The organization, as such, is thus: The first section is a discussion of some of the problems we have encountered and our solutions to them (pp. 10-49) , followed by a section presenting some knotting patterns, a few pieces illustrating how the techniques may be combined in a specific work (pp. 50-87) and pictures of a number of finished projects (pp. 88-107). The last section is a miscellaneous collection of technical information which may be useful (pp. 108-151).

SECTION

1

CORD LENGTH

Old-timers have told us that the cords for a belt must be four to seven times the length of the finished belt depending on the diameter of the cord and the tightness of the knotted pattern. With experience, the knotter is supposed to learn whether to use the ratio 4, 5, 6, or 7. But with experience, most people get tired of making belts and find that it's even harder to estimate the cord requirements for more elaborate pieces. There seems to be no reliable guide for estimating the length of cord needed to knot anything. The only way to gauge the cord requirements for a particular piece is to knot a sampler of the pattern, or patterns, to be used in the piece, take the sampler apart and measure the cord used for each inch or foot of the pattern, then multiply by the length of the finished piece. If the piece you want to make is one for which there are instructions available, the instructions will include the length of cord required.

Our approach to this problem is to avoid it. We cut all our cord into 14-foot lengths, which, when doubled, give working lengths of 7 feet. We have an old bed with posts seven feet apart, handy for cutting cord, because we can each use a side to cut cord at the same time. Cutting cord is perhaps our least favorite job, so we do as much as possible at a time and store it for later use. Fourteen-foot cords can be hung from a peg board or curtain rod in most rooms without touching the floor.

There is nothing sacred about the 7-foot working cord length. Recently we moved to an old New Hampshire farmhouse in which the ceilings are low, about 6½ feet, and we experimented with using 12-foot cords so they could be stored without dragging on the floor. It turned out, however, that the six-foot working length is not as good for larger projects and we have chosen to modify our storage to accommodate the longer cords.

Figure 1. Our work room and cord storage area.

What we did was to remove the ceiling in the living room so the headroom was increased by about one foot in the area between the beams. This method is a bit too drastic to recommend for other people who might have the same problem. A solution requiring less carpentry would be to double the cord, tie it at each end, and double it again to hang it (see Diagram 1).

Using cord of a relatively short standard length has another advantage: The shorter cords do not tangle as much as longer cords, and if tangled, they are easily unsnarled so that it is not necessary to bother with bobbins or butterflies or other methods of preventing tangles. Making bobbins is a waste of time better spent knotting.

1. Cord storage.

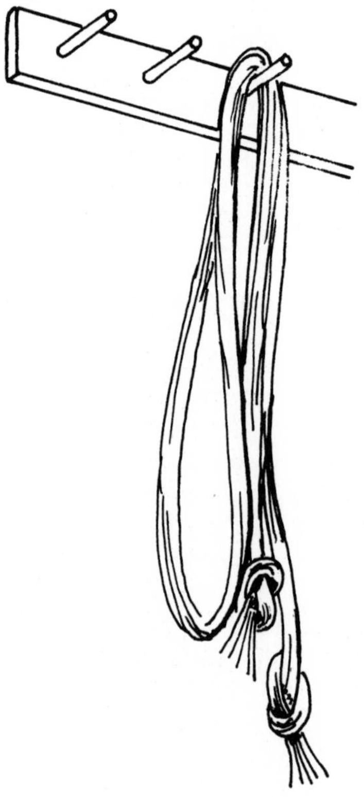

REPLACING SHORT CORDS

The next problem we encountered is immediately obvious. How do you replace cords which are too short to finish the piece? It is possible to splice cord, but we don't bother because it's too time-consuming. The four ways we use most often to replace short cords are shown in Diagrams 2-5.

All of these methods are most suitable for use in patterns which are densely knotted with a back side on which the short ends of the replaced cords will not show. If the piece is a lamp or circular hanging in which the inside will not be seen, no further finishing is needed, and the replaced cord ends are allowed to hang inside the piece. If the piece is to be viewed from both sides or if extra strength is required, the ends are secured with glue. Ordinary white household glue half diluted with water will dry to a strong transparent glue that will not discolor or stain the cord. Use plenty of glue and work it into the cord with your fingers. After the glue has dried for a few hours, trim the ends close and recoat the cut ends with glue to prevent unraveling. If the gluing and trimming of the cords is done carefully, the replaced cords will not be obvious. Some people like to hide short ends by weaving them back into the pattern.

As a rule, when there are many cords to replace, it's best to replace them at different levels in the pattern. If the cords are all replaced at the same level, there will be a visible line across the piece marking the replacement. Staggering the replacements will make the line less obvious. In some articles, the line of added cords is incorporated into the design of the piece so it doesn't matter if the line shows. All of the articles shown in this book were knotted with working cords seven feet or shorter.

ADDING CORD

As we will discuss later, cords are often added to a piece to increase the number of working cords rather than replace short cords. Increasing the number of working cords is done to widen a piece or increase the density of the knotted pattern. All of the methods in Diagrams 2–5 are suitable for the addition of working cords, and the cords "replaced" are simply continued in the work instead of being left out and trimmed off. There are, however, some other methods suitable for simple addition of cords, as shown in Diagrams 6–10.

2. Replacing cords two at a time (center cords).

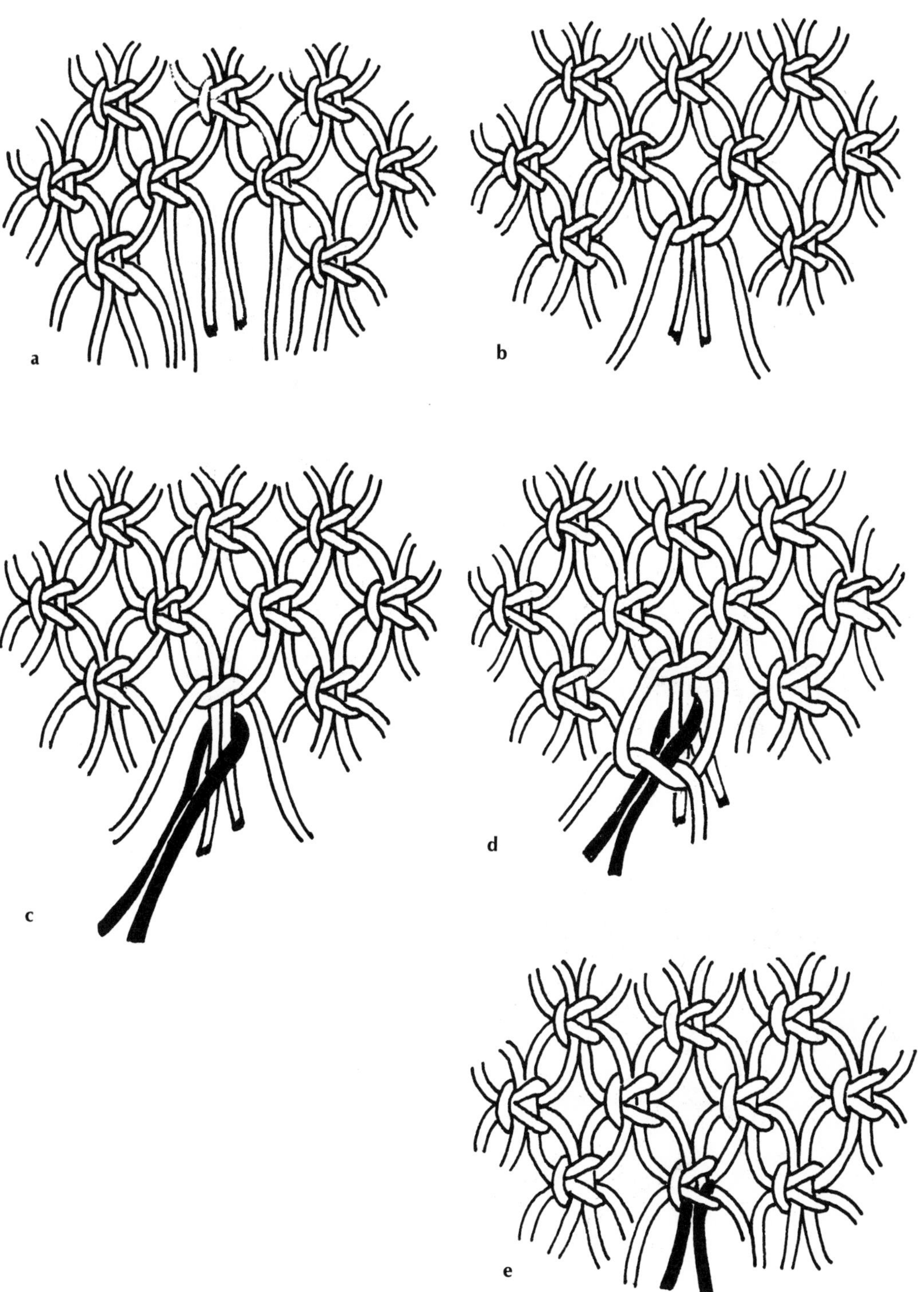

3. Replacing cords two at a time (edge cords).

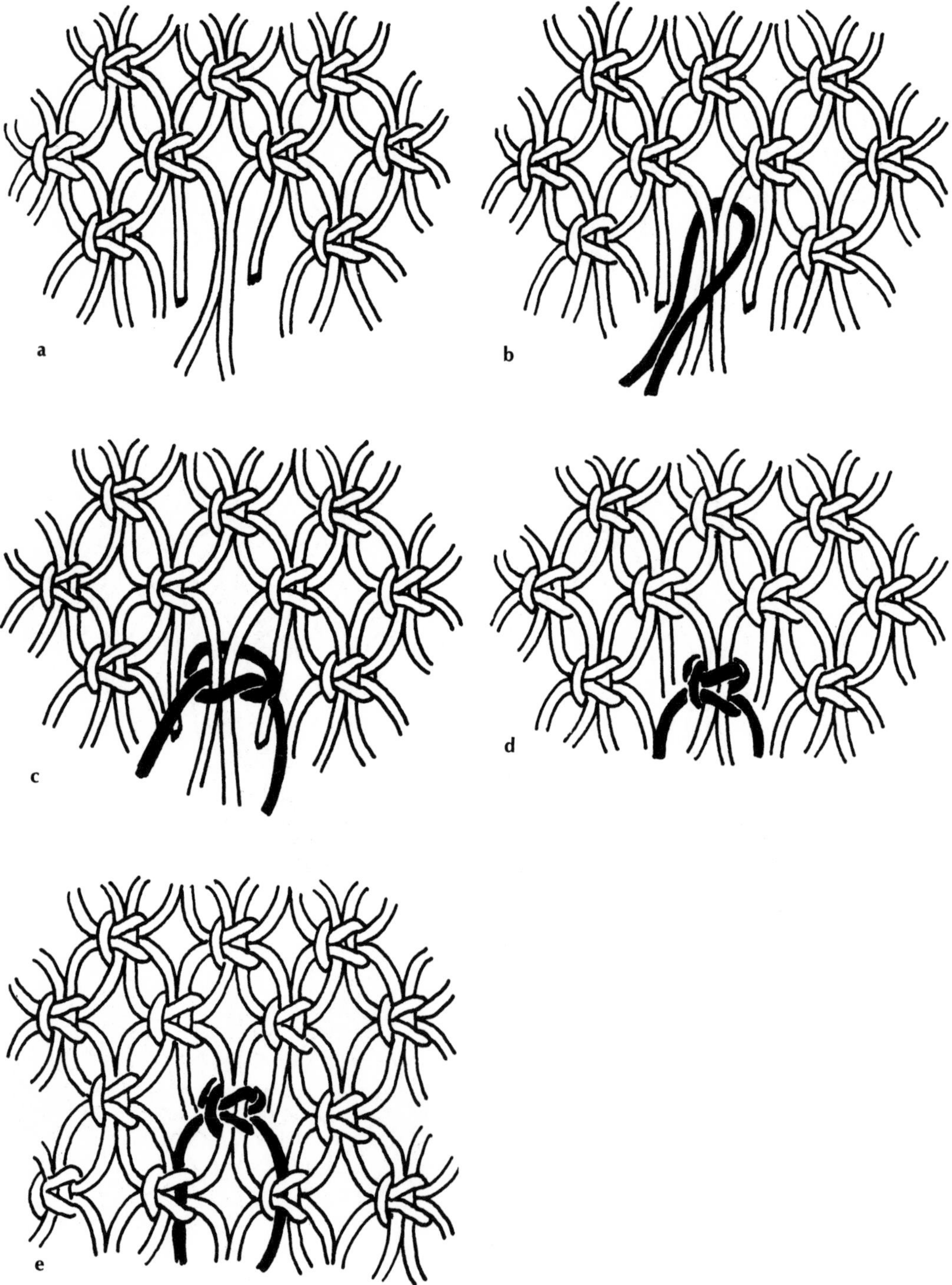

4. Replacing cords four at a time.

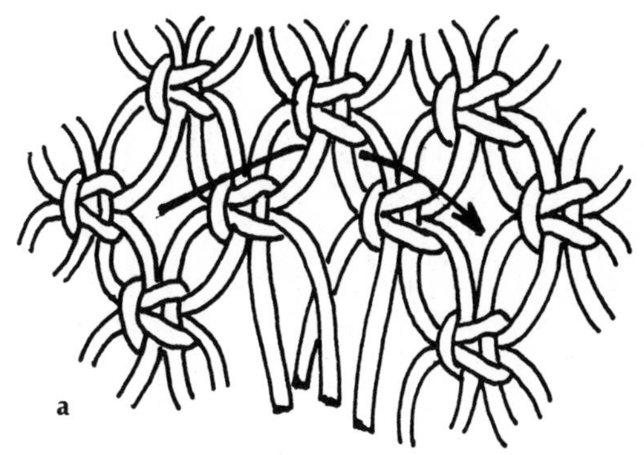

a

b

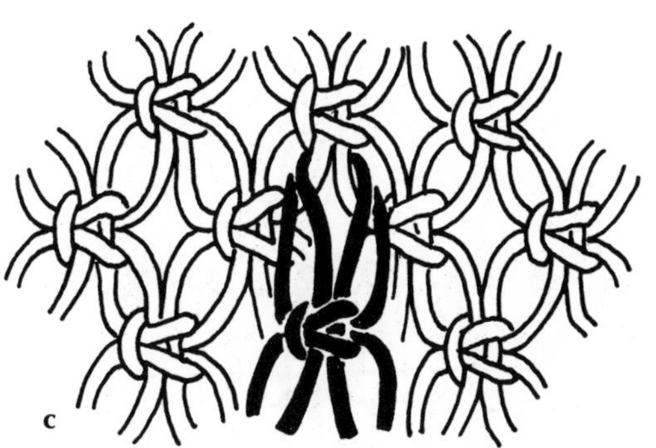

c

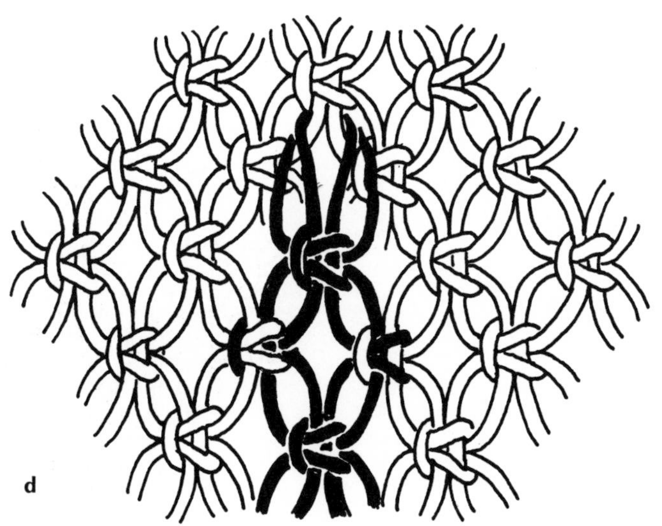

d

5. Replacing cords over a clove hitch edge.

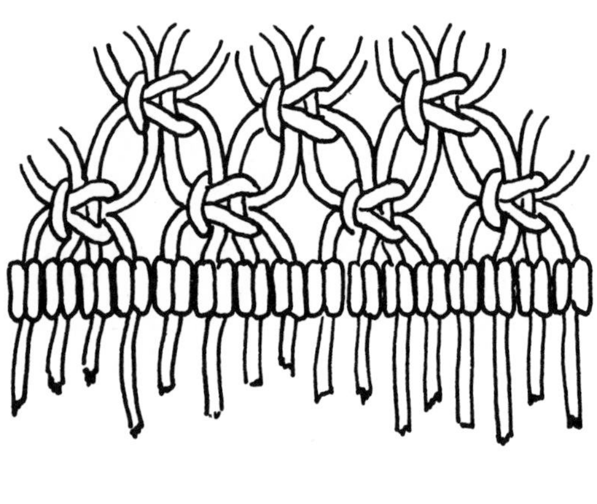

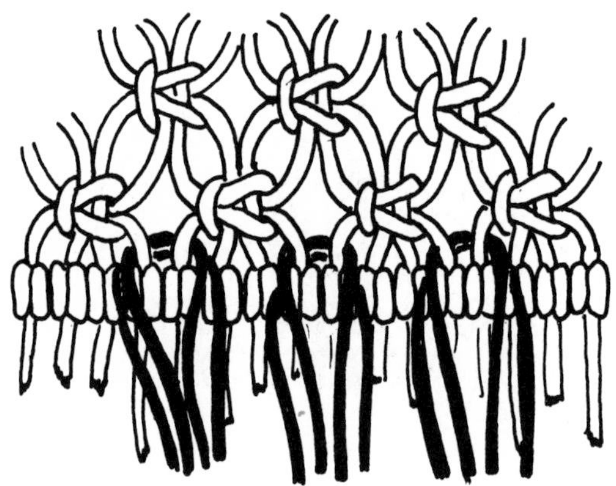

6. Adding four cords in two stages.

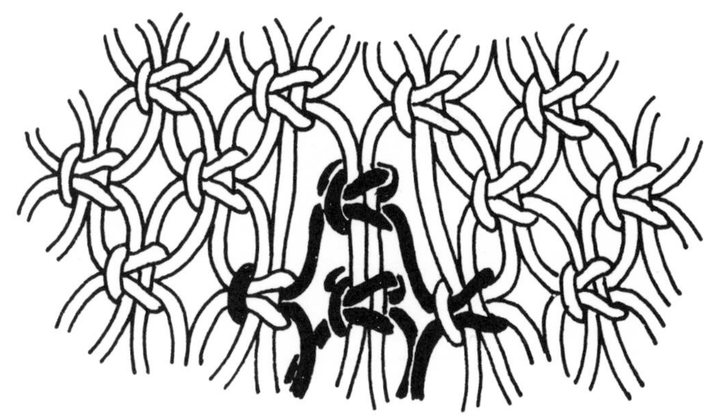

7. Adding cords to a free edge.

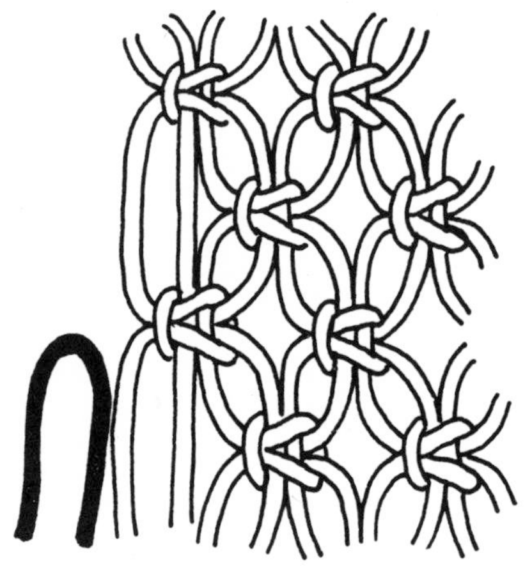

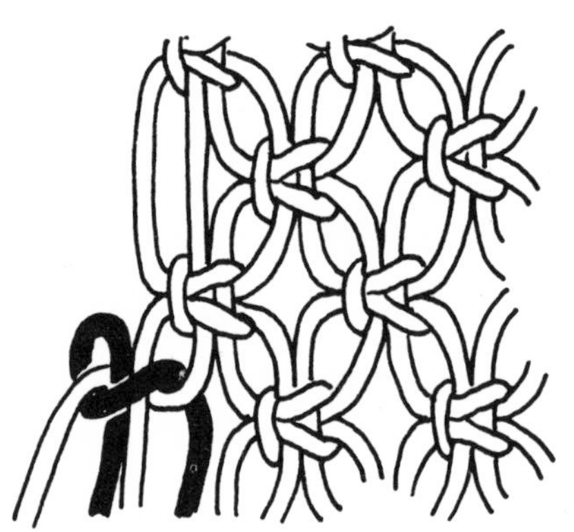

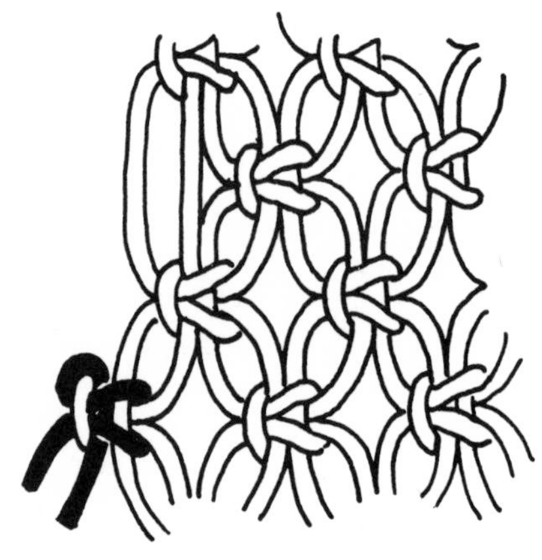

8. Adding four cords to a free edge.

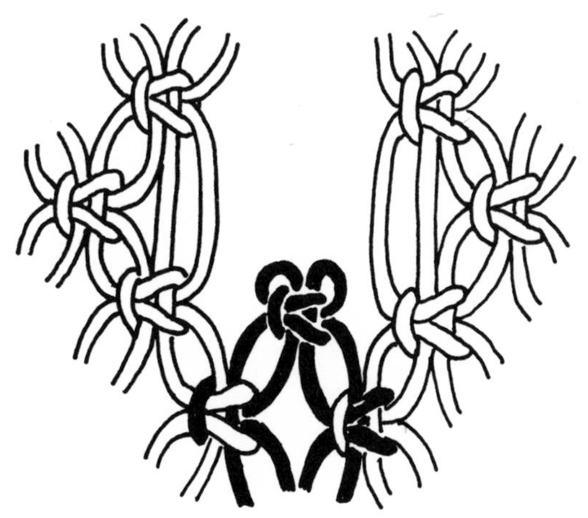

9. Adding four cords.

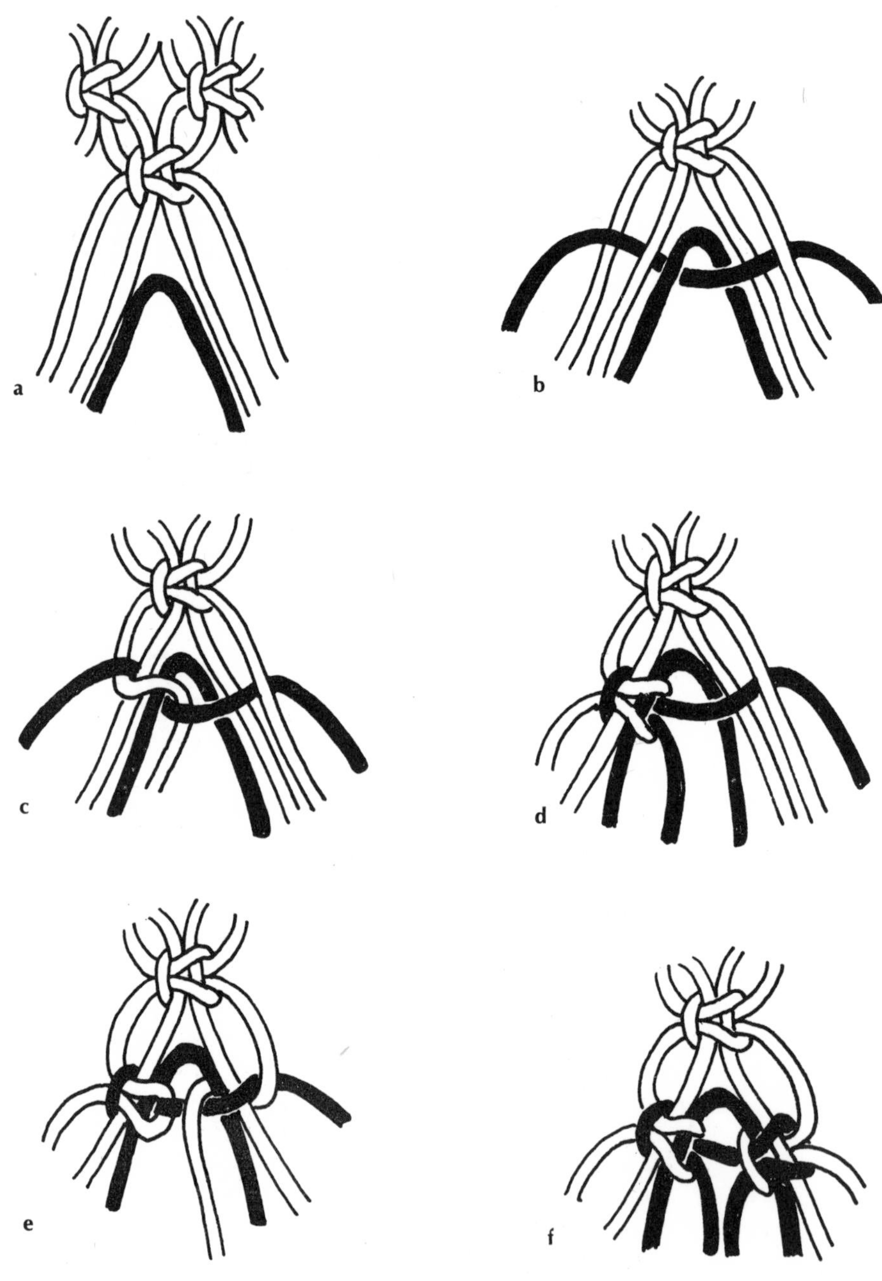

10. Adding four cords.

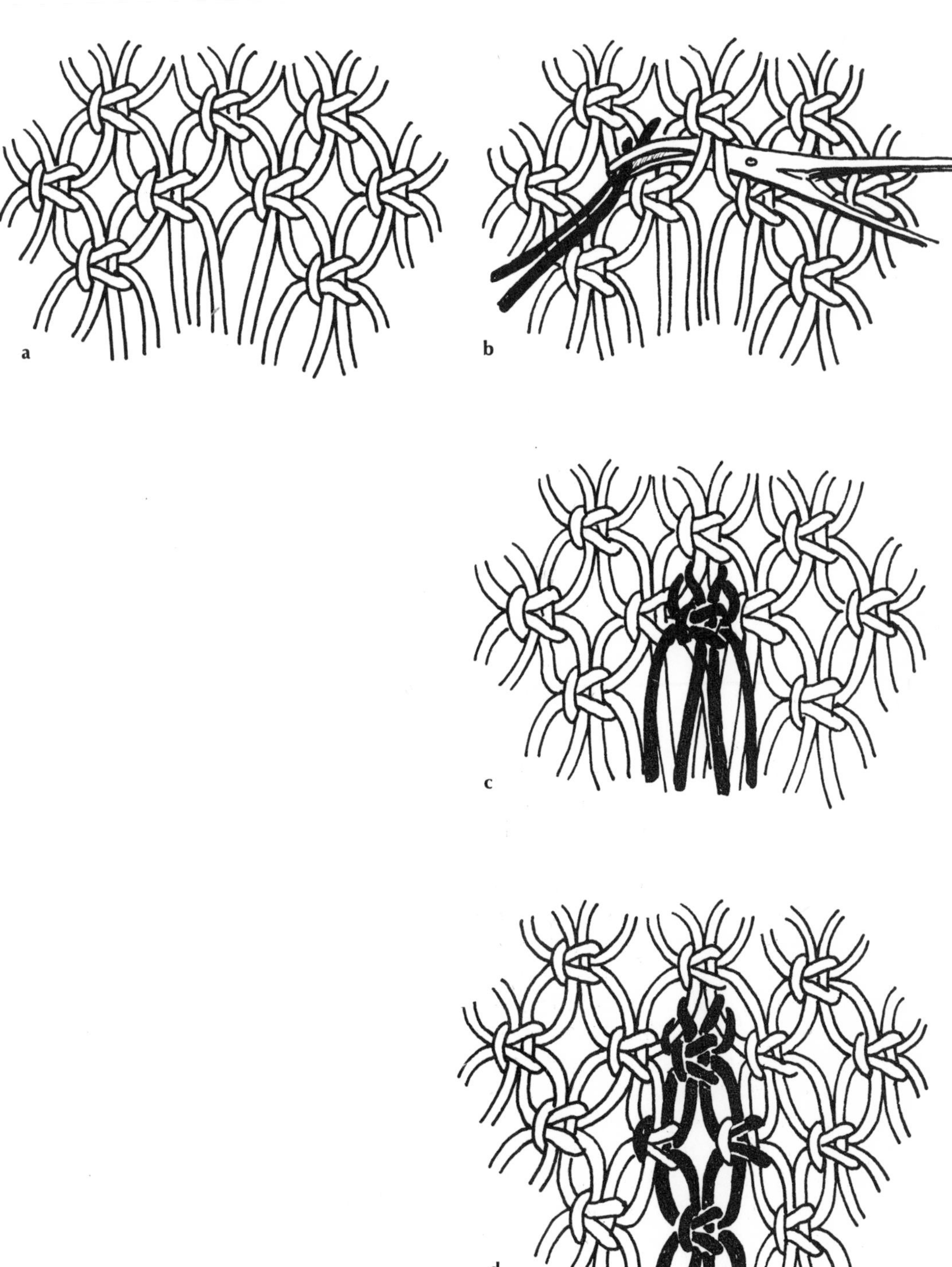

DELETING CORD

Creating shapes and sculptural forms with knotting requires that you be able to add and delete cords from your work. The best way to delete cord from a pattern is depicted in Diagram 11.

When deleting cords which will be added back in later, the cords removed from the pattern are carried along behind the knotting until needed. This is a technique very handy for making colors appear and disappear in a knotted piece. Cords are brought back into a pattern by adding them in a manner similar to adding new cords.

Most of the methods of adding and deleting cord are easiest and least obvious when used in a densely knotted pattern, such as the alternating square knot (see Diagram 12). After some experience, these and other methods may be used in more open patterns without being obvious.

11. Deleting cords four at a time.

12. Effect of adding (above) and deleting (below) cords in an alternating square knot pattern.

TYING BOARDS

As you can see from the things we made, we don't work much on tying boards. Tying boards are fine for flat pieces such as purses or vests, but they are restrictive and completely unsuitable for more elaborate three-dimensional projects. If you want to make the sort of knotted articles shown in this book, you must learn to work without tying boards.

If you have learned to do macrame on clipboards with pins to hold the cords in the pattern and keep the pattern even, you will have to relearn to tie the knots securely and evenly without any such aids. The best advice for anyone wishing to do advanced projects in macrame is to throw away T-pins, clipboards, belt clips, or bobbins and learn to tie knots without them. You will find that knotting is faster and freer when you have dispensed with these encumbrances. For example, when clove hitching a number of working cords over a carrier cord, it's easiest and fastest to hold the carrier cord in one hand and tie the clove hitches with the other hand. If you are working from right to left, hold the carrier cord in the left hand and tie with the right; when working from the left to the right, hold with the right and tie with the left. As you work you can control the angle of the carrier cord with the holding hand and shape curves or angles with ease. It's easily twice as fast as bothering with a tying board and pins and can be done when working on a piece hanging in front or above you, which it would be impossible to do using a tying board.

Figure 2. Tying boards should be used only for flat pieces such as vests and purses.

PHOTO SERIES A

When tying clove hitches, hold the supporting cord in one hand and tie with the other. As you can see, shapes obtained can be determined by the angle at which the support cord is held.

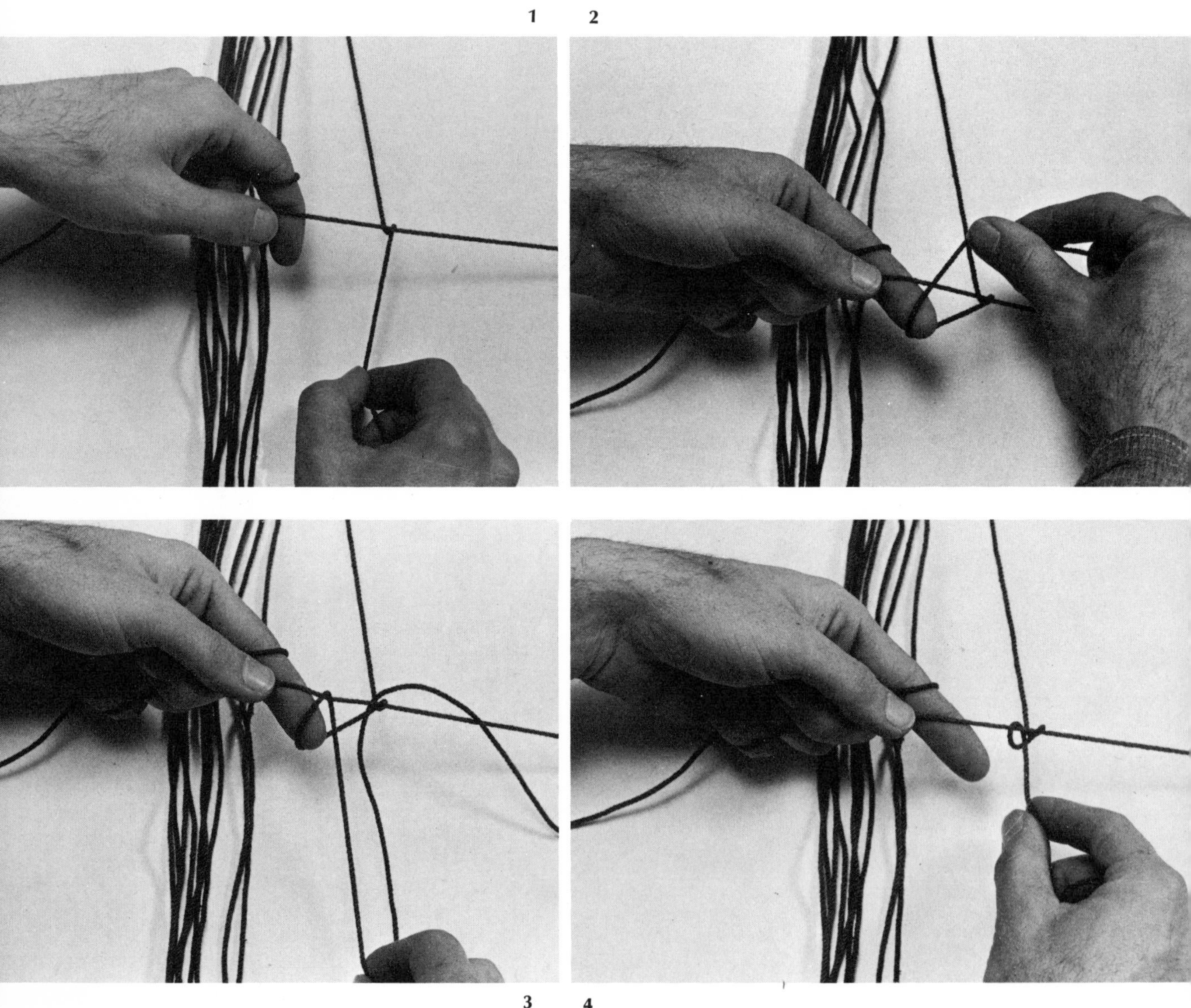

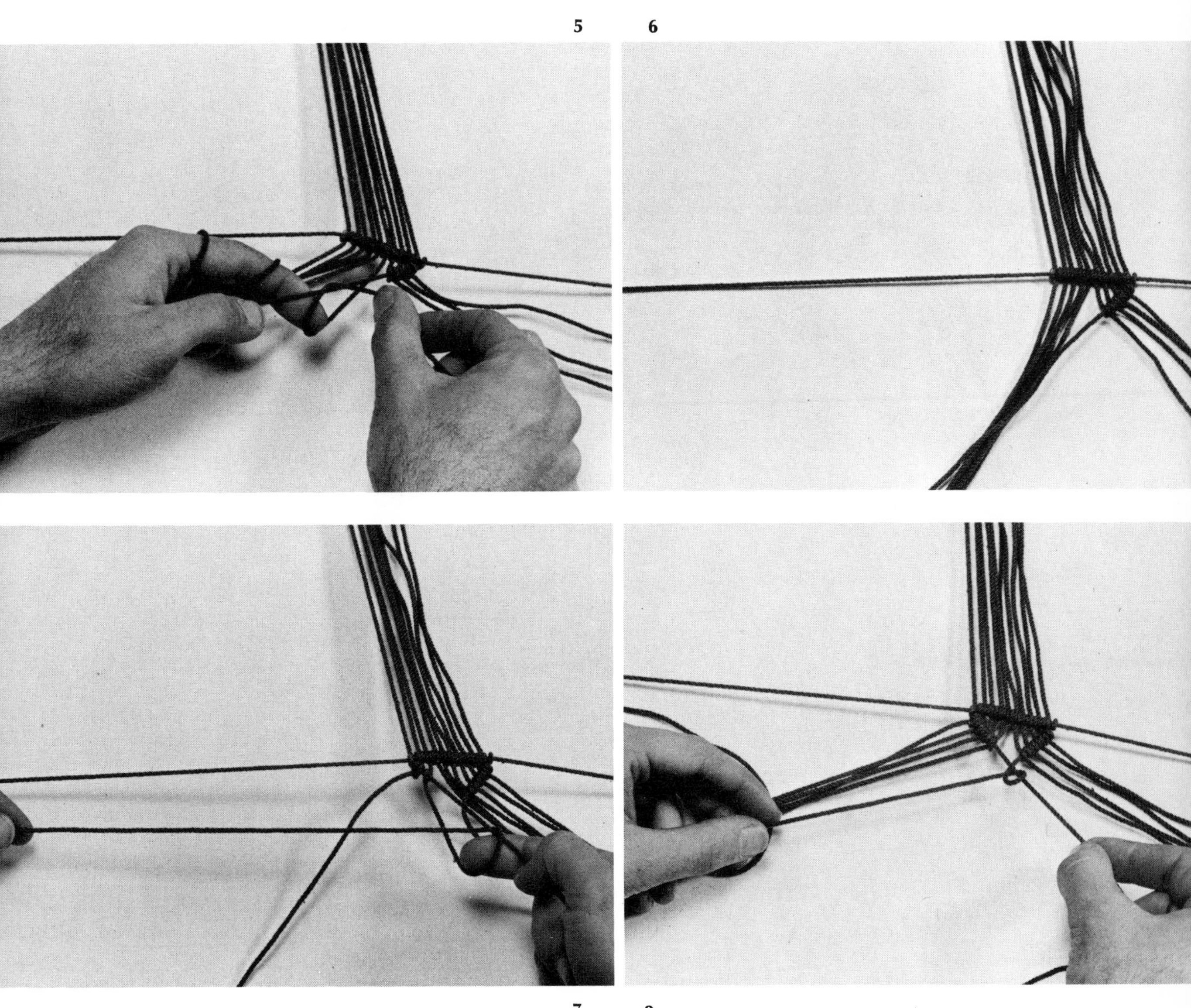
5 6 7 8

9 10

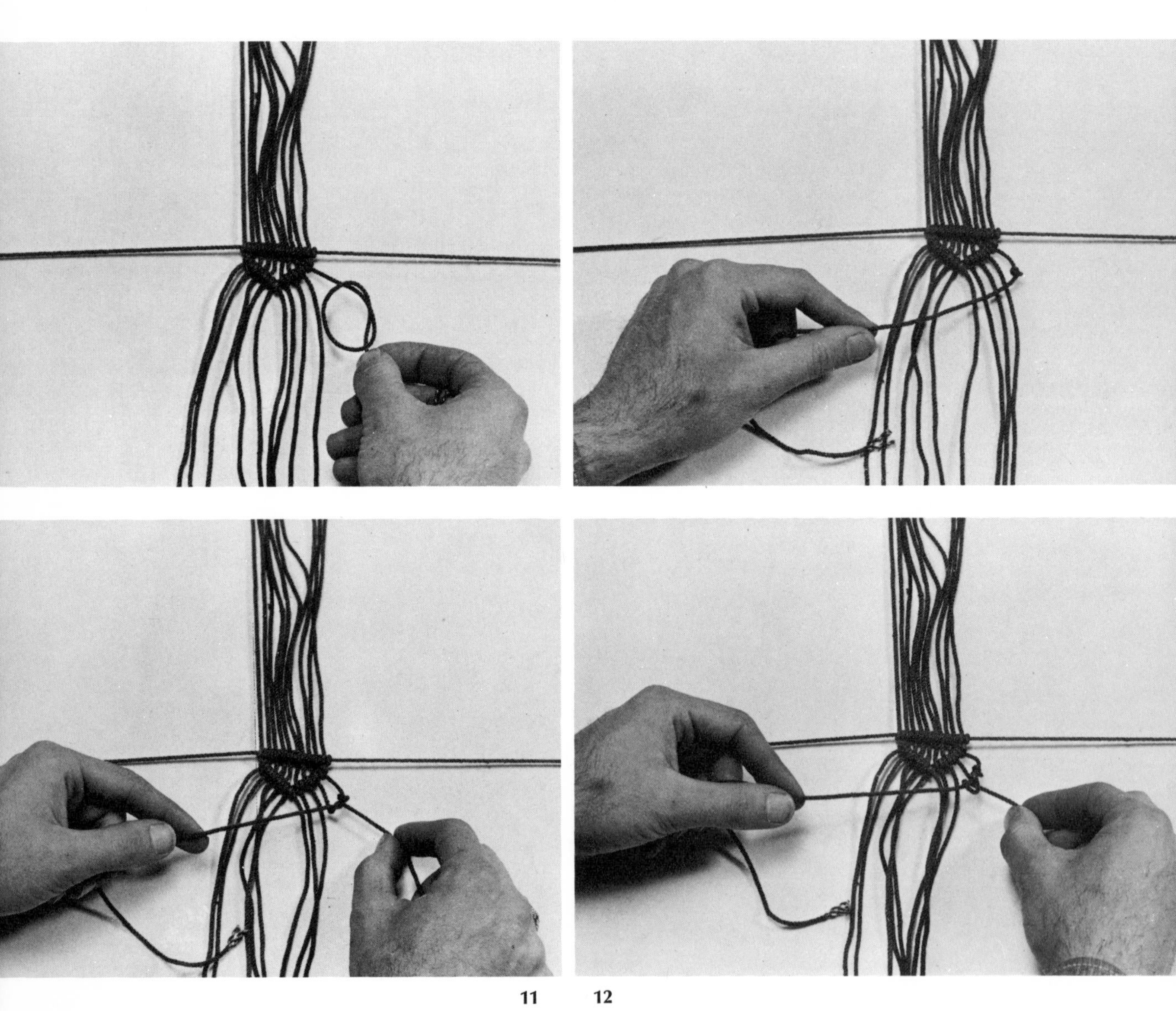

11 12

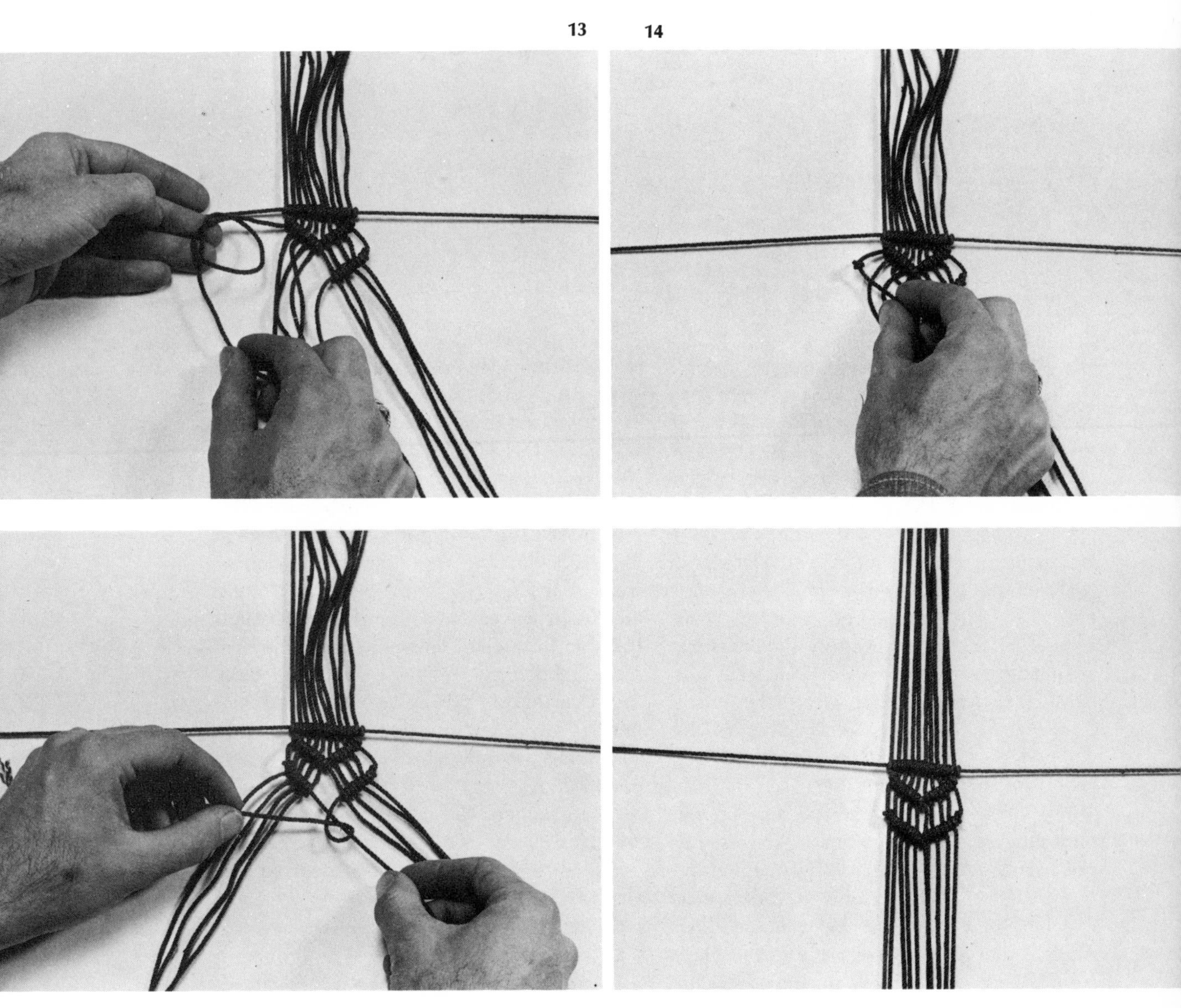

13 14

15 16

MACRAME DESIGN

There are two basic approaches to making something in macrame. The first approach could be termed the *logical approach*. In this method of knotting, you begin with a plan of the piece to be done, generally a fairly detailed sketch, in which the knotting patterns to be used in each part of the piece are indicated. From the plan, the piece is analyzed and broken down into its component parts. After consideration of the plan and its analysis, any necessary modifications are made before the project is started. The knotting is begun and the piece takes shape in a sort of reversal of the analysis as the components are knotted and assembled. We never use this method.

The other approach to macrame is the opposite or *illogical approach* and is our preferred way of working. In this method the project is first begun, often with only a general idea of what it will be when finished. Most of the decisions are made as the piece is tied. If someone has asked us for a specific item, we may start on that, or on something needed for the house, such as a lamp or a chair. That's about as much of a plan as we ever have, and usually we just grab some cord and start. This way of working requires that you have some precut cord always on hand, for nothing stills the creative urge so quickly as cutting large amounts of cord. We also like to have some wire frames on hand as well as beads, bells, and rings. But if there aren't any frames handy, we start without them and make the frames later, if they are really needed. Sometimes a lamp will grow into a swing, or a hanging will look better upside down, but usually we end up with something pretty much like what we had in mind. An occasional project will require some sort of planning. The chair and cradle shown on pages 99 and 93 were first sketched in order to have the frames made, but the sketch was only of the framework; the knotted patterns evolved as the piece was tied.

If you have some experience in knotting—a belt or two is enough—we would recommend the second approach to you. It's more fun than planning and lets you spend your time knotting instead of drawing. At first you may have to force yourself to be spontaneous in your work, but you will find the results more satisfying and uniquely your own. Don't worry about creating a monster; we haven't lost a project yet.

The only drawback to this rather disordered approach to knotting is that your home or workshop will reflect the disorder. Some sort of cord storage area is needed as well as an area where you can leave partially finished projects hanging, standing, or lying about until you get back to them. Our living room looks like a cross between a spaghetti factory and a commando obstacle course. If your family is intolerant of your mess, you'll have to appropriate a spare room, the attic, or the garage for your work.

Whatever area you work in should have several ceiling hooks or other means of supporting a hanging or lamp while you are working on it. Our living room has exposed beams that we can drive nails into wherever needed. It's an old house, so we use antique nails. But most people have ceilings that you can't drive nails into, which is one reason we recommend the attic or the garage where you'll be able to hook cords to the rafters or rafter ties. If no other means of hanging a piece is available, make a frame of 2" x 4" lumber like the one shown in Diagram 13.

Never hang a work in progress from a light fixture. It's dangerous. Many of the pieces we work on weigh enough to rip a light fixture apart.

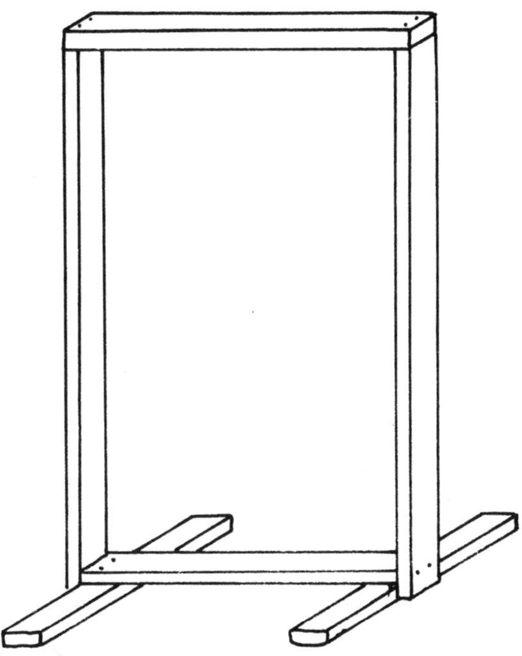

13. Frame for hanging pieces while working on them. It's approximately six feet high and three feet wide.

When working on a large piece, it's best to work standing up so you can move around as required. Motion is important in tying even if the finished piece is static, for as you move when working on the piece, your motion will be transferred to the design. With precut cord hanging over your shoulder, scissors and hemostat in your pocket, you're ready for anything. If you don't have a hemostat or don't know what it is, Figures 3 and 4, 5, 6 on the opposite page demonstrate the hemostat and its use.

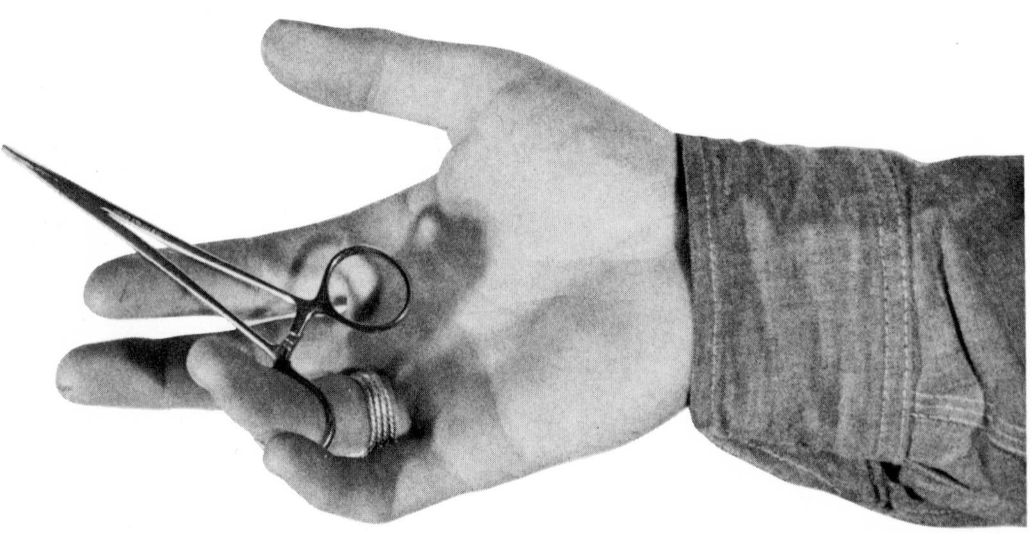

Figure 3. The hemostat.

Figures 4, 5, and 6. The hemostat is useful for getting cord through tight places.

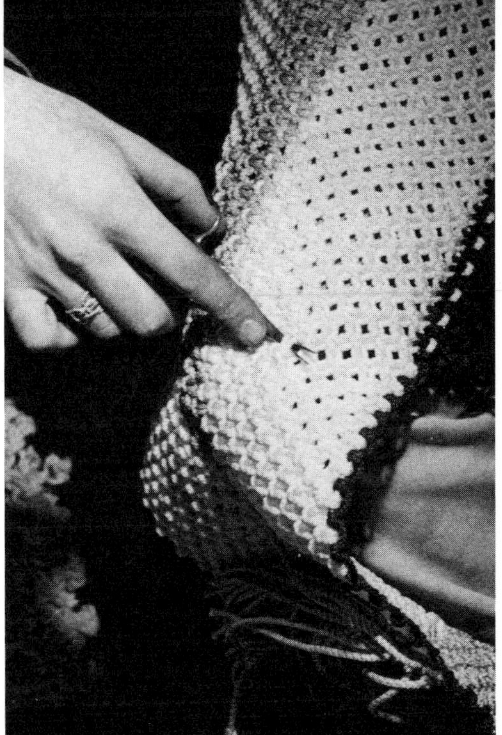

4

5

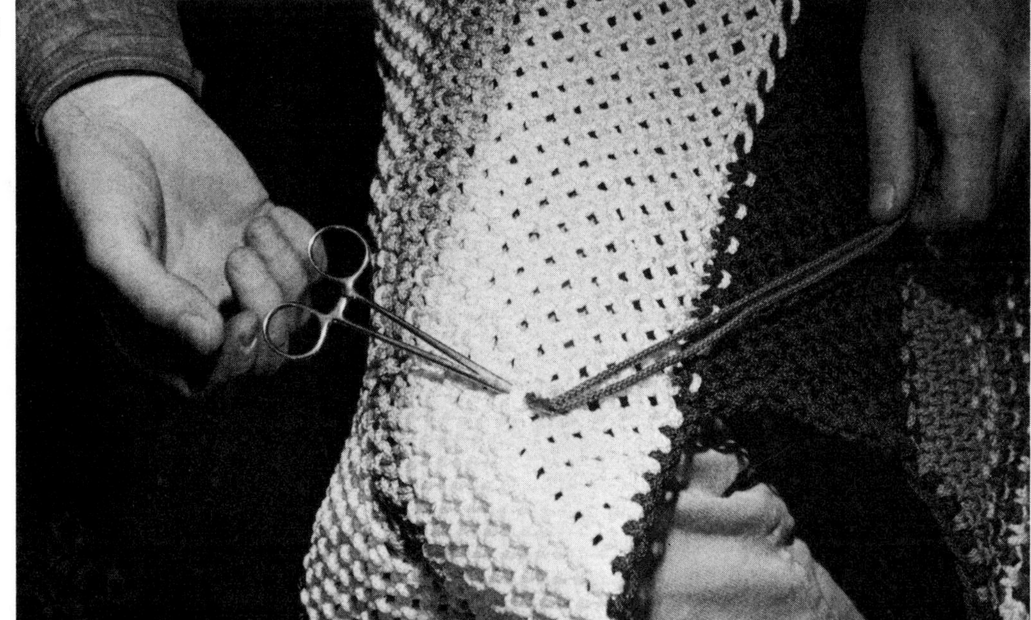

6

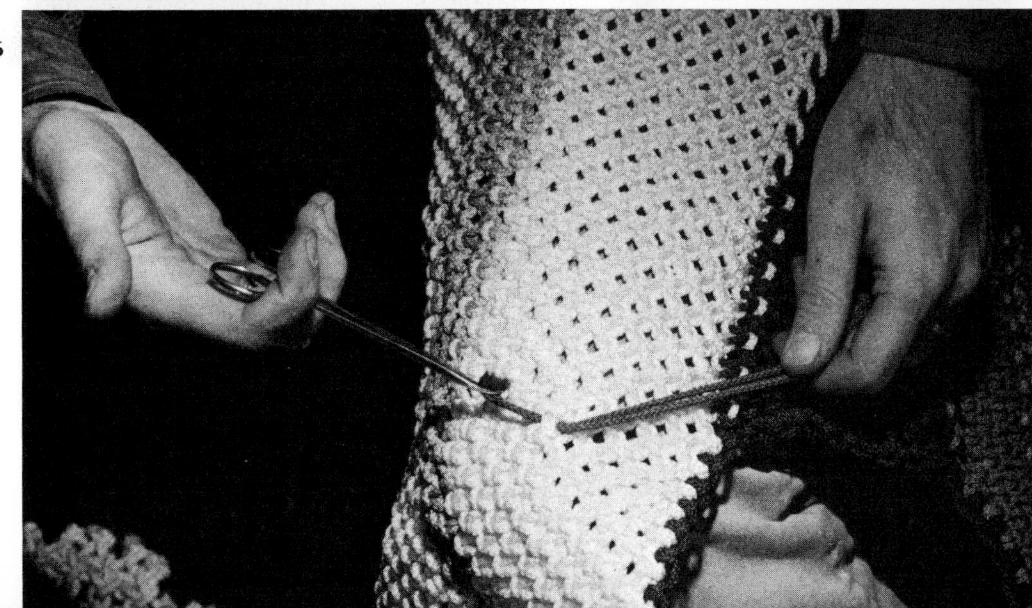

TYPES OF CORD

Cord is chosen for a specific project for many reasons, including its cost, color, texture, and availability. With the current interest in macrame there is greater variety of cord available than a few years ago. But many of the cords offered are not ideal for knotting and some are practically useless. Following is a brief guide to the selection of cord for macrame, based on our experience and reflecting our personal preferences and prejudices.

Cord may be made from natural or man-made fibers. In all cases, the fiber characteristics determine the type of cord which can be made from it as well as the appearance, texture, and strength of the finished cord.

Cotton, linen, wool, and the hemp family of fibers are the natural fibers most used in macrame. Silk can be used, but it is expensive. Natural fibers are relatively short and must be spun or twisted into yarns to provide material of sufficient length to make twine, string, rope, or cable.

Man-made fibers, on the other hand, can be produced in indefinite lengths. Twisting or braiding of these fibers is done not to obtain greater fiber length but to create cord of a particular finish and strength to fit its intended use.

Cord may be twisted or braided into its final form. The older method of making cordage was to spin fibers into yarns, then twist yarns together into small cords, small cords into large cords, large cords into rope, and ropes into cable. Many cords suitable for macrame are twisted cordage. We use twisted cord because we feel that the knotting looks better; one of our favorite types is cotton seine twine. It is available in sizes from 1/32" to ¼" in diameter, is relatively inexpensive, and dyes readily with Rit or Tintex dyes.

Cotton seine twine is made by several manufacturers and the quality will vary somewhat. The size number of the twine gives the number of yarns twisted together to make the cord. Number 18 cotton seine twine, for example, contains 18 yarns while number 240 has 240 yarns. The larger the number, the larger the size of the cord, but No. 36 is not twice the diameter of No. 18, since doubling the number of yarns does not double the diameter of the twine. Cotton cable cord is similar to seine twine but is made from coarser yarns so that cable cord of a given size will be larger than seine twine of the same size. In general, we have found that cable cord is of poorer quality than seine twine and we encourage people to go to the bother of locating a supplier of seine twine whenever possible.

For most small projects made with cotton seine twine we use sizes 24 to 54, and larger sizes (120 and up) for furniture or architectural pieces. Cotton seine twine may be easily spliced and looks good in combination with other natural fibers, or with glass and ceramic articles. The larger sizes, however, are hard on the hands and somewhat more difficult to handle. Whenever strength and weather resistance are needed, it is better to use one of the synthetic cords developed for nautical work if you can, since cotton will deteriorate fairly rapidly upon exposure to the elements.

Nylon seine twine is also twisted cord sized by number to correspond to the sizes of the cotton twine. Nylon twine is made up of many minute fibers twisted into cords and it therefore tends to unravel rapidly as you work with it. The smooth surface of the cord allows knots to slip so that more care is required in its use. Nylon twine can be dyed with Rit or Tintex by simmering the dye bath for about one half to two hours, depending on the shade required. Once dyed, nylon twine is almost completely colorfast to cold-water washing and to light, unlike cotton which fades with washing and exposure to light.

To prevent unraveling of nylon twine we melt the ends of the cord with a propane torch. If done carefully, the cord will not discolor in the flame and the twine will not unravel.

There are two types of braided cord: Solid braid and hollow braid, as illustrated in Diagram 14. Solid braids are generally used in smaller-size cord. Hollow braids consist of an outer braided cylinder with an inner space which often contains a core of straight, twisted, or braided fibers. Most braided cord is made for the surface characteristics of the braid. Braided cord has a smoother, more decorative surface, is easier on the hands and offers more resistance to kinking than ordinary twisted cord. It is the cord of choice for use on pleasure sailing craft.

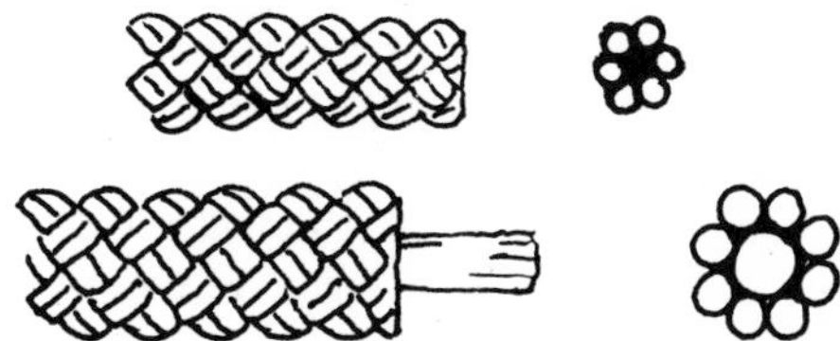

14. Hollow braid (above) contrasted with braid containing a core of longitudinal fibers (below).

There are three synthetic fibers which are most often used for making braided cord: Nylon, Dacron, and polypropylene. All three are also used to make twisted cord and most marine supply houses will have each fiber available in cordage of various sizes in both twisted and braided form. Each type is designed for a particular use aboard a boat and if you want to work with these cords, you should know something about the characteristics of each.

Nylon cord is strong but will stretch up to about 20 to 25 percent of its length without breaking. If you were making a swing or chair bottom of cord, you wouldn't want to use nylon because of the stretching. However, for clothing, such as a vest, the stretching may aid in fitting and increase comfort. But in large garments, the weight of nylon may be objectionable.

Dacron cord is also strong and does not stretch much. It would be the ideal cord for use where stretch of the cord would not be acceptable, as in making a swing. It is about as heavy as nylon.

Polypropylene cord is strong, stretches little, and is very lightweight, but not as resistant to chafing as dacron. Lily Mills Co. makes a polypropylene hollow braid called Macra-Cord which is very good for macrame. This cord has a great deal of body and may be used to tie unsupported shapes that cannot be tied with other types of cord. Because of its light weight, Macra-Cord polypropylene is good for clothing, but its stiffness prevents it from making good fringe.

Larger braided cord usually has a core of twisted or braided fibers. This inner core is not dyed when the outer braid is dyed, so when a piece is ended, it's often a problem disposing of the undyed inner filler cord. One method is to slide the covering braid back on the core, cut the core off short, and slide the cover back down beyond the core (see Diagram 15).

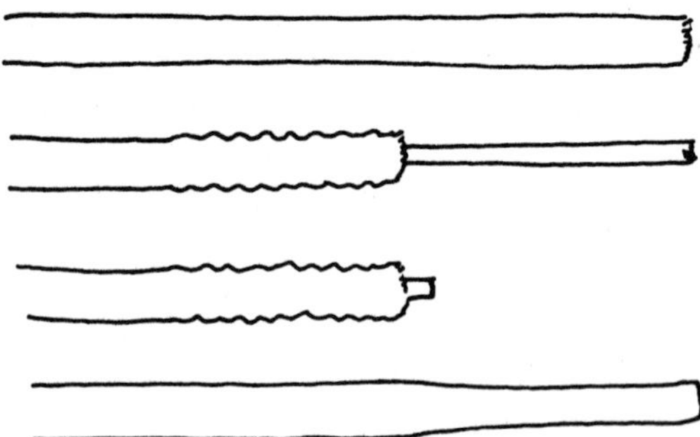

15. In order to finish braid with a core, slide the outer covering back a few inches and trim the core short so it will not show in the completed work.

Recently, a braided nylon seine twine was introduced. Sized by number like the twisted cord, it is useful for macrame, but in the larger sizes has a core of fibers that is difficult to dispose of. Most braided cords with a fiber core were designed to be resistant to kinking, and are therefore difficult to tie into tight knots. A knot is a form of kink in a line and any cord resistant to kinking is therefore resistant to knotting.

There are other specialty cords offered by suppliers which aren't very suitable for macrame. Most houses carry a "macrame cord" which is usually a soft-twisted cotton cord about the size of number 12 cotton seine twine. This fine a cord is practically useless for anything except small belts, necklaces, and the like. Naval cord is a hard-twisted, polished cotton cord that has long been the favorite of sailors. It is suitable for traditional work in the nautical style of macrame but not very useful for most of the more elaborate things we do. Rattail cord is a soft, highly ornamental, expensive hollow braid which is practically useless, although a favorite of necklace makers.

Yarn and fuzzy cords such as jute twine can be used for macrame but we find that the texture of the yarn obscures the knotting in most pieces.

One of the most important considerations in buying cord is its price. Most of the less expensive cords aren't very good for macrame. Of the cords we use, cotton seine twine is the cheapest and it's pretty expensive. Nylon seine twine is about twice as expensive as the cotton and the various specialty cords are even more costly. When making large objects, you will find that the cost of the cord can become prohibitive.

The best place to look for cord is a marine supply house or marine hardware store. Stay away from the places catering to the yachtsman; you'll probably find more suitable cord and better prices at the dock-side firms serving the commercial fisherman. Several years ago, most fishermen began using nylon twine for netting and it's become hard recently to find good quality cotton seine twine.

DYEING YOUR OWN

With so many supply houses presently selling dyed cord of different fibers and finishes, perhaps few people will be interested in dyeing their own material. We still do some of our own dyeing because we can get the exact colors we want and save money.

We use Rit and Tintex dyes and do the work in our kitchen. Cotton cord is washed first, to remove dirt and grease; nylon can be dyed as it comes. The cord to be dyed is made into hanks containing up to one pound of cord and presoaked in hot tap water. The dye is combined with hot tap water in plastic dish pans for the cotton cord and enameled steel buckets or steel dish pans for the nylon. When the cord has been soaked thoroughly in the hot water, it is transferred to the dye pan and completely immersed in the dye bath. We let the cotton cord soak for a few minutes to an hour and simmer the nylon on the stove for thirty minutes to two hours depending on the shade desired. The dye bath should be stirred and the cord turned about every fifteen minutes so that the cord will be evenly dyed. We get more mileage from the dye by dyeing several shades of each color. For example, Tintex Dye's Sunflower Orange will dye nylon a light silvery yellow in 1 minute, light yellow in 2 to 3 minutes, yellow in 10 to 12 minutes, yellow orange in 30 minutes, and a deep orange in 1 to 2 hours. Also, by starting with the lighter colors and adding other colors you can mix your own shades as you go. A typical operation would start with light and medium yellow dyed from yellow dye, then light green from the addition of a small amount of medium blue, and finishing up with a greenish bronze color obtained by adding a light brown dye. We have dyed as much as 40 pounds of cord in a few hours with one helper making the hanks for us.

If you're going to do your own dyeing, it's better to stick with one brand and learn the characteristics of each color you use, since results will vary from brand to brand. The hardest colors to dye colorfast are the dark ones: brown, red, blue, green, and black. If you can buy them ready dyed, do so and dye your own lighter colors at first. Later you can try the darker shades.

After dyeing, we rinse the cord in gallons of cold water until the rinse water is clear. If the cord is to be used in clothing, we also wash the cord in warm soapy water several times and repeat the cold rinses.

Although it sounds like a lot of work, home dyeing is easy and may be used on cotton, nylon, or jute twine with good results.

FRAMEWORK

Most cords used in macrame have insufficient body to hold certain shapes, such as spheres, without special techniques in knotting or some supporting framework. Although cord can be made self-supporting by treating it with varnish or plastic (as will be discussed later), it's generally easier and faster to use some rigid supporting framework. For relatively simple circular hangings and lamps, there are many rings and hoops available for use. We spend hours browsing in hardware stores and marine supply houses looking for new cords and new hardware. Probably our best find was the lamp shade holder shown in Diagram 16.

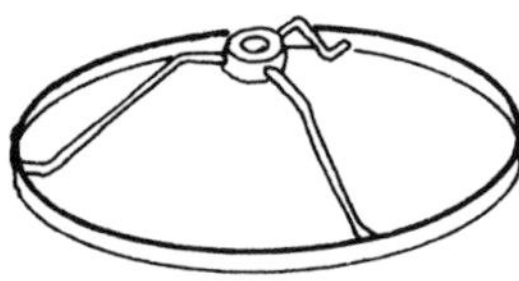

16. The lampshade holder is useful for macrame pieces.

Lamp shade holders come in various sizes, from about 6 to 18 inches in diameter, and make ideal supports for knotted lamps. The outer rim supports the macrame and the inner hub is bolted to a socket for the electric light. The three spokes can also be used in the knotted pattern. An appliance repair shop or electric lighting service store should have lamp shade holders as well as other necessary fittings for making lamps. Threaded brass tubing in various lengths is used to fasten sockets to the hub of the shade holder and can also be used to bolt together several shade holders for more elaborate lamps (see Diagram 17).

The same stores should also have a selection of lamp bases and fittings to hold chimneys and globes—all of which may be useful in making knotted lamps (see Diagram 18).

Metal pieces used in macrame are sometimes best made to fit the work in progress. Fabrication of metal parts is a field of knowledge too extensive to discuss in detail, but with practice the knotter or hobbyist can master a few simple techniques and will find them useful.

17. Two or more lampshade holders may be bolted together.

18. Lamp bases, globes, and chimneys are used in illuminated hangings.

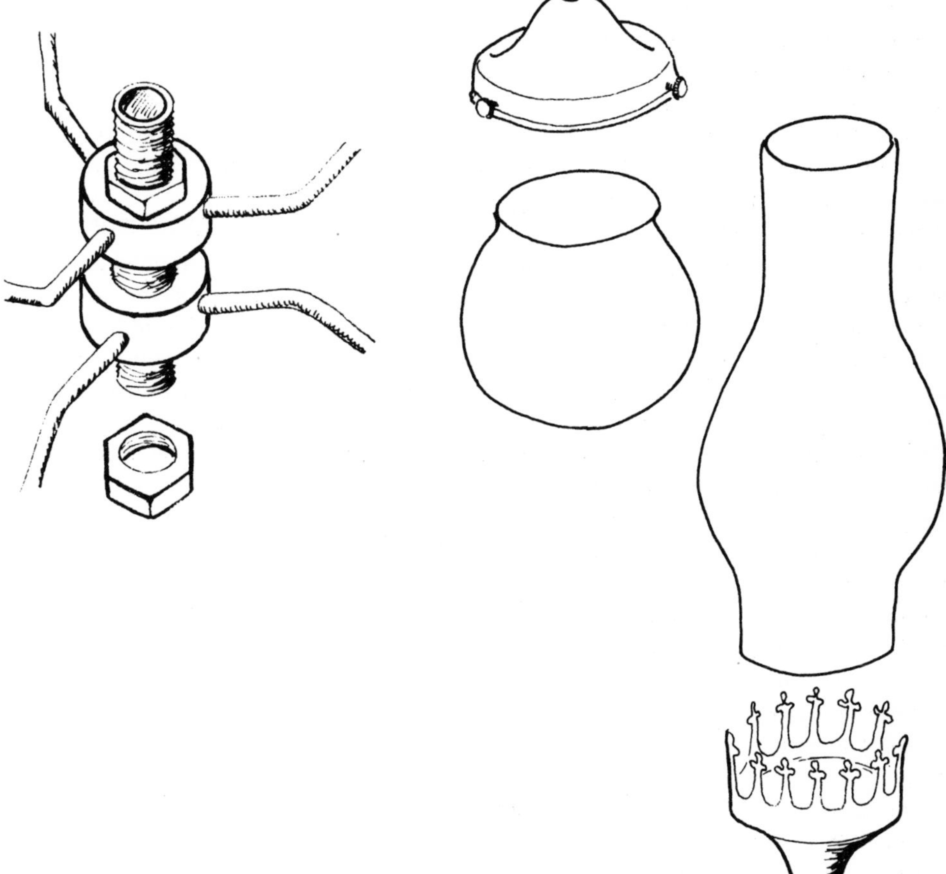

Metal parts can be joined in many ways. A mechanical joint is easily obtained by bolting or wiring metal pieces together. This method is obvious and needs no explanation; unfortunately it is of little use in macrame.

Physical bonding of metal parts is the preferred way of making metal frames for macrame. There are many methods used today, only a few of which are available to the amateur. *Soldering* involves a bonding of two metal parts by the use of another type of metal, usually a lead alloy, which is flowed over the joint while molten and then allowed to cool. There are many solders available with widely different melting points and flowing characteristics. When brass brazing rods are used to make frame pieces, they may be soldered together. When soldering, there are a few rules to follow. The metal to be joined must be scrupulously cleaned and in mechanical contact, a proper flux must be used, the metal heated, and a proper solder applied. If you haven't had experience soldering, your hardware dealer can recommend a suitable torch, a soldering iron, flux, and solder for you to use. With practice, soldering will become a fast and easy way to fuse brass rod; it is not practical for use on steel or aluminum.

Brass and steel rod used for frames can be fastened by *brazing*. In brazing, the metal pieces to be joined are heated nearly to their melting point so that the superficial layer of molecules is molten. Then the second metal is added and melted so that it actually mingles with the superficial layers of the metal being brazed as the joint cools. Brazing requires much more heat than soldering and is only slightly stronger than silver soldering, but it can be used on steel. For brazing steel you will need a gas and oxygen torch, brass brazing rod, special flux, safety goggles, and expert instruction.

The strongest way of fastening metal is *welding*. In welding, tremendous heat is applied and the area of the joint is actually melted together by the addition of flux and extra metal during the melting process. Welding is a good way to join steel parts when great strength is needed, but it requires expensive equipment. Most communities have a welding shop or mechanic that can do the welding for you at a nominal price.

Scrounging is still the best way to find interesting frame members for your work. If you want to make a macrame chair, you could use the frame from a discarded butterfly chair (see Diagram 19). If you don't have an old butterfly chair rusting in the garage, Sears or Penney's can provide a new one for about ten dollars. You could also use an old wooden chair with a broken-out cane seat (Diagram 20). If you want to work on such a chair, you can probably find one in a local

19. The frame from an old butterfly chair is a good start for a macrame chair.

20. The seat of a caned chair can be replaced with knotting.

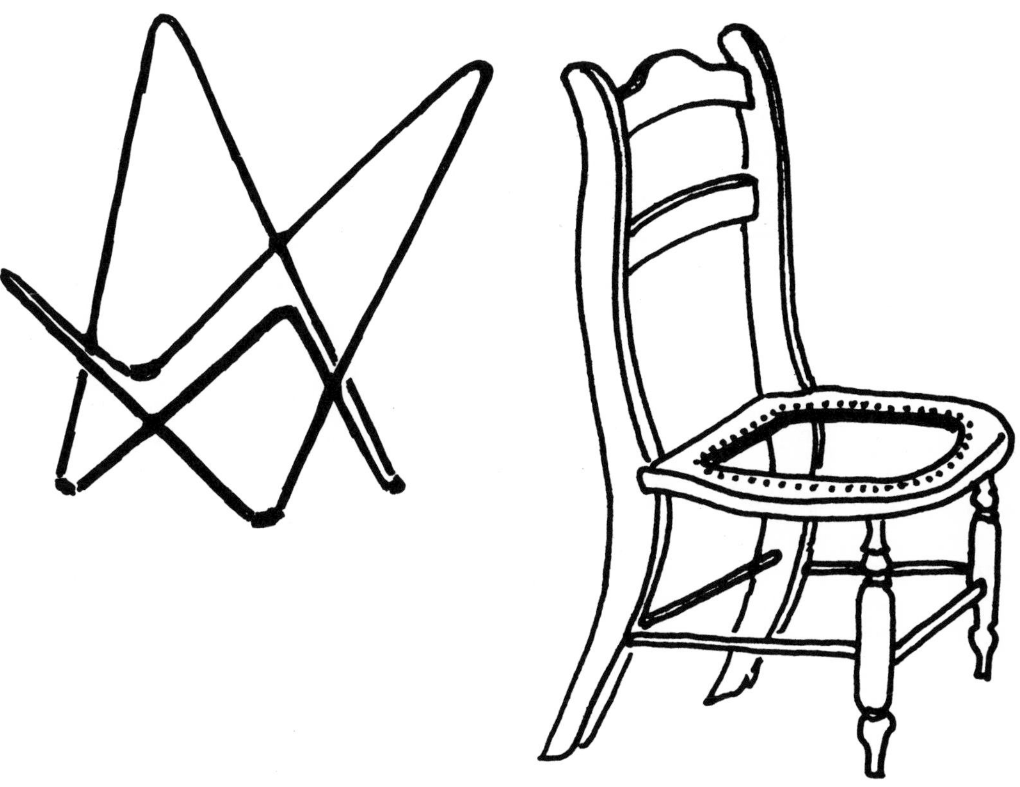

junk shop. But if you buy an old chair for this purpose, remember that there are two types of cane-bottomed chairs. The older chairs were hand-caned in a series of weaving steps, with cane strips passing through holes in the rim of the seat. This sort of cane chair would be very suitable for use with a macrame seat, and is the one shown in Diagram 20. Later, caned chairs were not handwoven, but were caned by installing a piece of machine-woven cane mat. This type of caned chair has a groove around the rim of the seat instead of holes, and is not suitable for use with a macrame seat, because there is no way to secure the cord to the chair. Do not attempt to convert this type of seat to the older type by drilling holes in the groove, because the chair will thus be weakened, and the wood will split with use. Chairs with cloth webbing or woven rush seats may be easily used for macrame seats (Diagram 21).

We used an old iron tire from a broken hay rake wheel as the large hoop in the swing on page 94. If you wanted to make a circular swing and you didn't have an old wagon wheel, you could make a rim of welded steel rod. Hoops from a barrel would be suitable for a small child's swing. We often adapt the project to the materials at hand rather than going to the trouble and expense of making frames for every article.

There are many wooden pieces usable in macrame, such as old banister posts, turned chair parts, or driftwood. "Natural forms" in macrame and the crafts in general have been popular lately, and you may wish to incorporate various "found objects" in your work. Seashells, rocks, or junk are inexpensive items you may use, but be careful with them, lest the finished piece end up looking like something better thrown away again. There are now many supply houses offering ceramic beads, bells, and other items for use in macrame hangings, and we have mentioned a few of these in the list of suppliers at the end of the book.

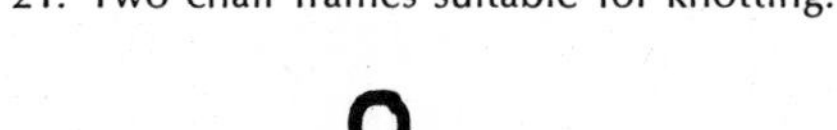

21. Two chair frames suitable for knotting.

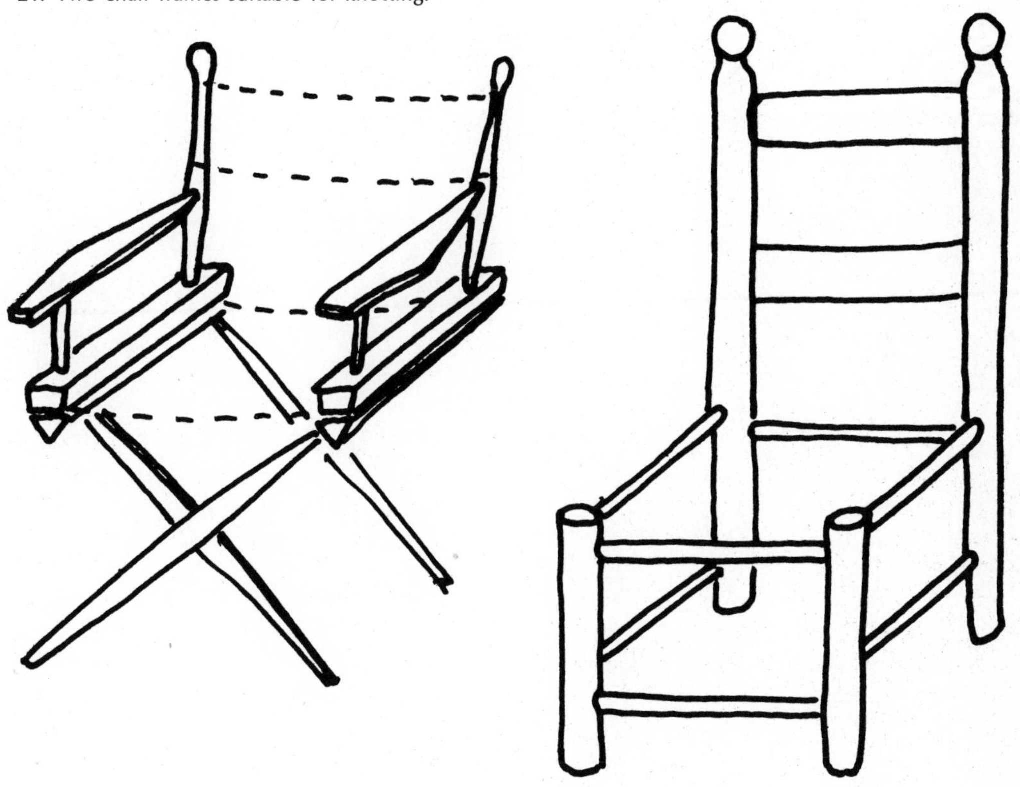

SECTION

2

22. Three ways to start a piece without framework.

KNOTS

Starting Patterns

Many macrame pieces can be started without using a frame piece as a support. You can begin a hanging with a single doubled cord, for example, and add cord by the methods mentioned in Section I until the piece has grown to include the required number of cords.

Flat or three-dimensional circular hangings may be started in several ways (see Diagrams 22 and 23).

When starting with lark's heads over a ring, we use a spacer cord and hide the ends as shown in Diagram 24.

If we start over a rope or cord, we sometimes splice the ends of the supporting cord together or make a cringle. But usually we just hide the ends of the support cord within the knotting (Diagram 25).

23. Two methods of starting a circular piece.

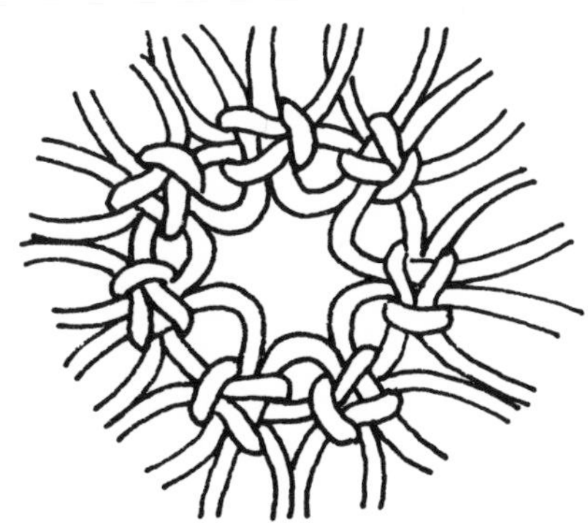

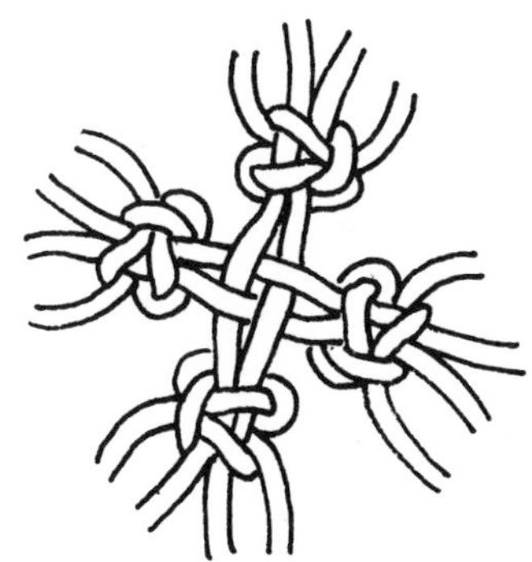

24. Use a spacer cord when starting with lark's head knots to maintain even spacing. The ends of the spacer cord are hidden as shown.

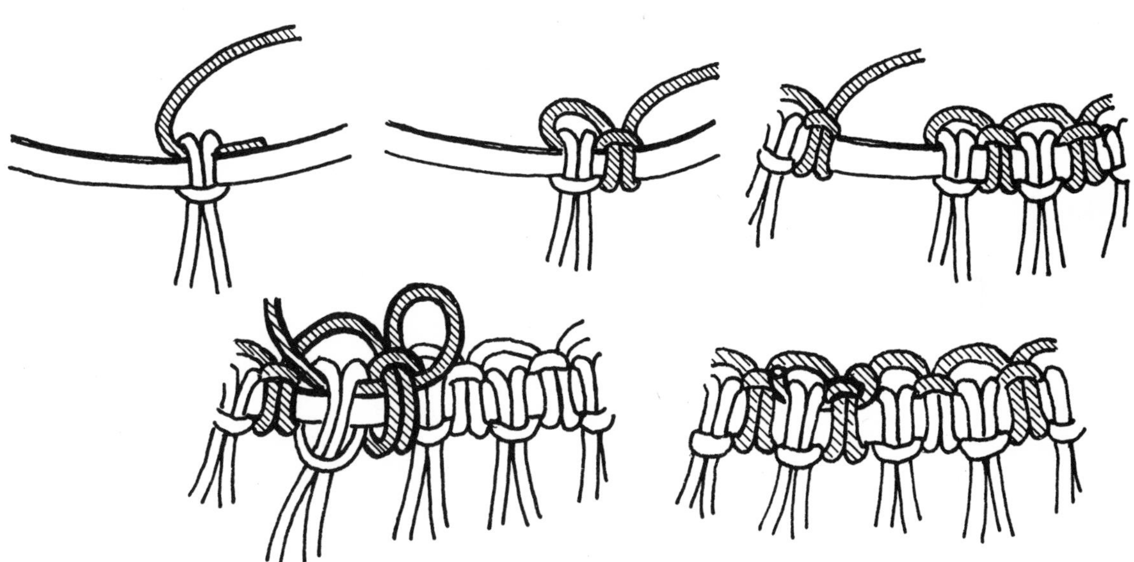

25. Starting with a cord used as the supporting member.

26. The alternating square knot pattern compared to the basket weave pattern.

27. Basket-weave variations.

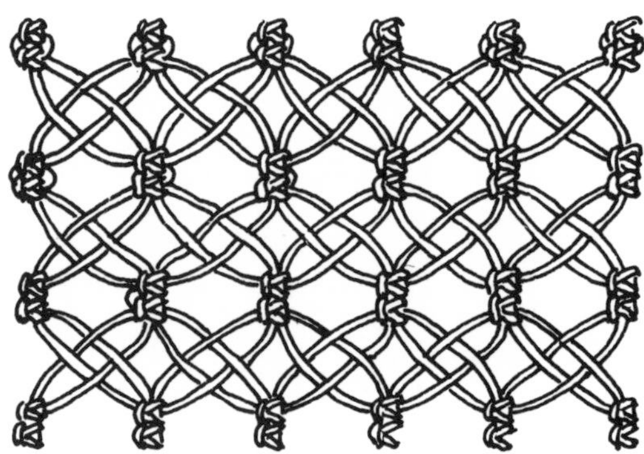

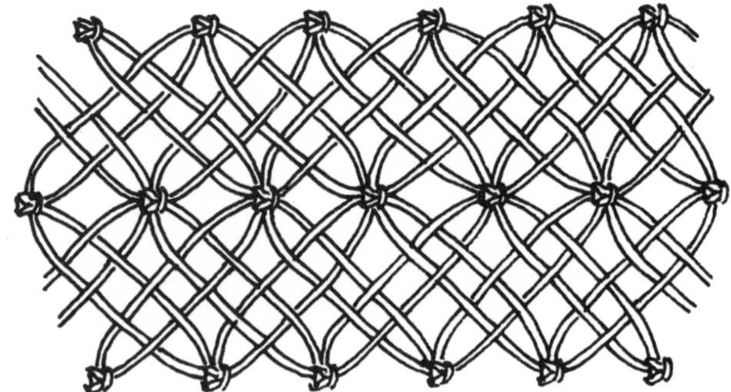

Working Patterns

Most patterns we use evolve as we tie them, but there are certain combinations which are particularly useful in different circumstances.

The basket weave pattern was first used in clothing. It is based on the alternating square knot pattern, but ties faster, uses less cord, and has more give and stretch than its parent. In the basket weave pattern, every other row of square knots is replaced by simple over and under weaving of the cords (Diagram 26). This pattern may be varied almost indefinitely (Diagram 27), and may be used to tie small areas within a field of alternating square knots (Diagram 28). As you create working patterns of your own, try using straight cords. In some pieces, large areas of straight cords with only few knots can be very effective (Diagram 29).

28. Basket weave combined with alternating square knots.

29. Patterns may also be created with a minimum of knots.

30. Left-handed and right-handed square knots.

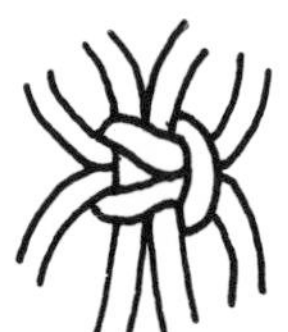

31.

32.

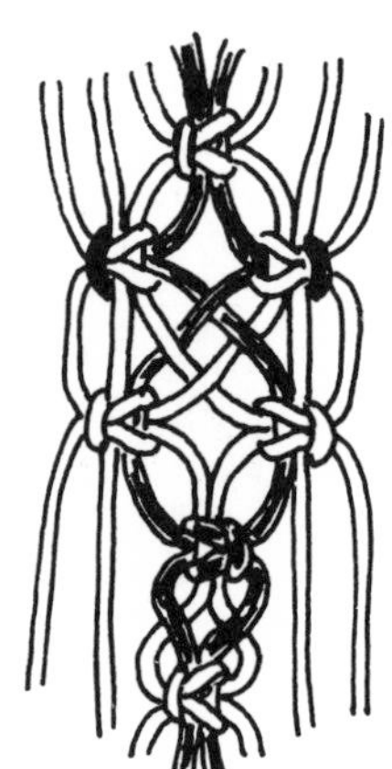

33. The type of square knot used at a color boundary affects the appearance of the finished piece.

Symmetry

The macrame square knot may be tied left-handed or right-handed. The knot is the same except that one is a mirror image of the other (Diagram 30). In many cases, it hardly matters whether a square knot is tied left-handed or right-handed, but when tying certain patterns and when working in colors, the piece often will look better if tied so it is symmetrical. To illustrate, look at a simple pattern tied two ways, first with only left-handed square knots (Diagram 31), and second with the pattern knots arranged symmetrically around the center of the pattern (Diagram 32). Elaborate patterns generally look better when tied symmetrically.

When working in a closely knotted alternating square knot pattern, you can also make designs in square knots of the opposite type, which will stand out against the background of the other type of knots.

Square knotted pieces of several colors require attention to the type of knot used in the areas where the colors abut. In the simplest case, a border between black and white cord, the type of knots used will make a difference (Diagram 33). Patterns using many different colors of cord are more complex, and careful choice of the knots is necessary. For example,

34. Different appearance results when different square knots are used.

35. Contrasting colors may be hidden by knotting over them to make the color appear and disappear through the pattern.

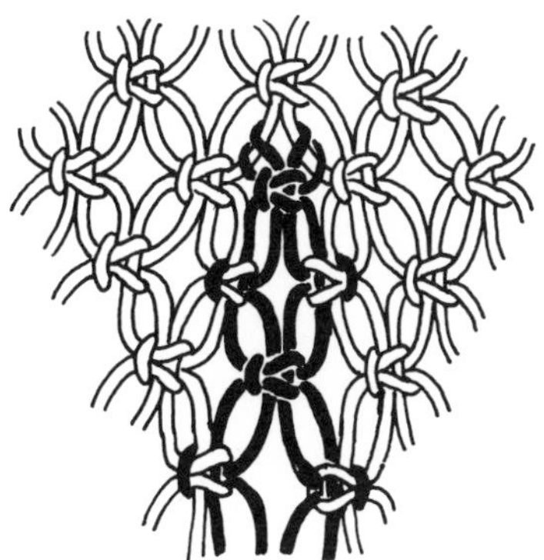

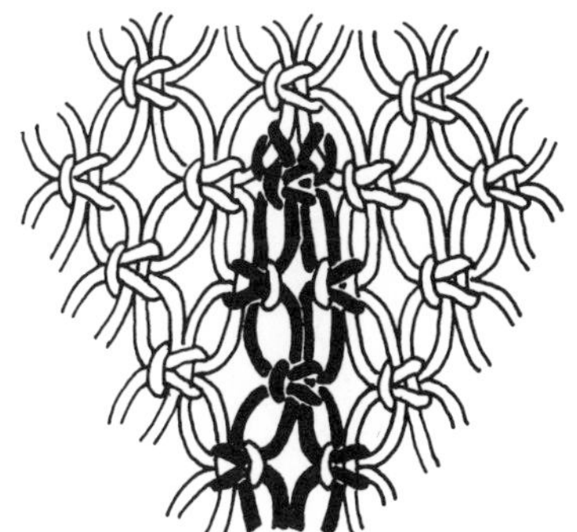

if four black cords are added to a piece in white cord, the type of knots used will affect the pattern (Diagram 34).

Contrasting cords added two at a time may be hidden and made to disappear and reappear in the pattern (Diagram 35).

In the nautical style of macrame, the clove hitch was often used when knotting belts and other such items. Knotting a flat band of clove hitches is similar to weaving in that certain cords run the length of the piece (as warp threads), with a second set of cords running across them (the weft). Diagram 36 shows a simple design based only on clove hitches. If the lengthwise or vertical cords are one color and the crossing cords another, it is possible to tie a two-color design. When the vertical cords are hitched over the crossing cord, the color showing will be that of the vertical cords and vice versa. Two-color designs are created by hitching one or the other cord, depending on which color is to appear. Multiple-color designs can be created by using a multicolor warp and weft, much the same as in weaving. Even complex plaids are possible. The *Encyclopedia of Knots and Fancy Rope Work* by Graumont and Hensel has good coverage of this type of work.

36. Clove hitching with vertical cords of one color (black) and horizontal cords of a contrasting color (white). By varying the direction of the clove hitches used, one or the other color will show.

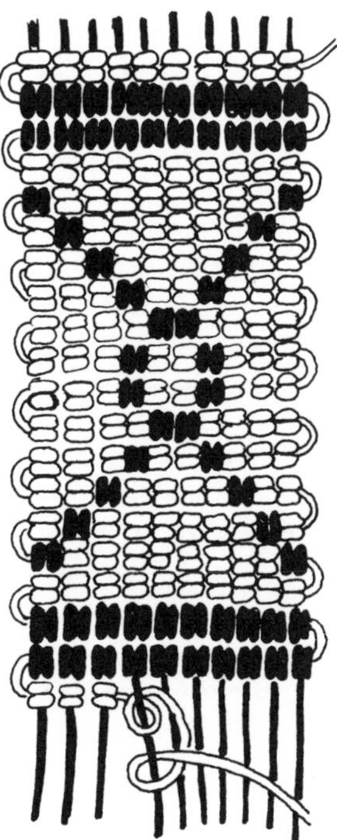

37. Ending knots: the overhand wrap knot (top) and the pear knot (below).

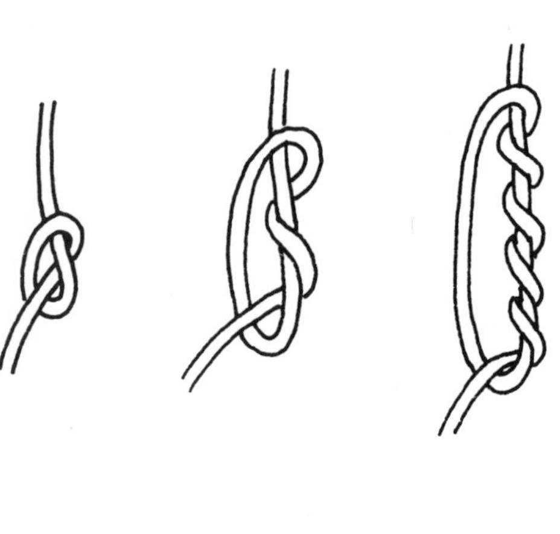

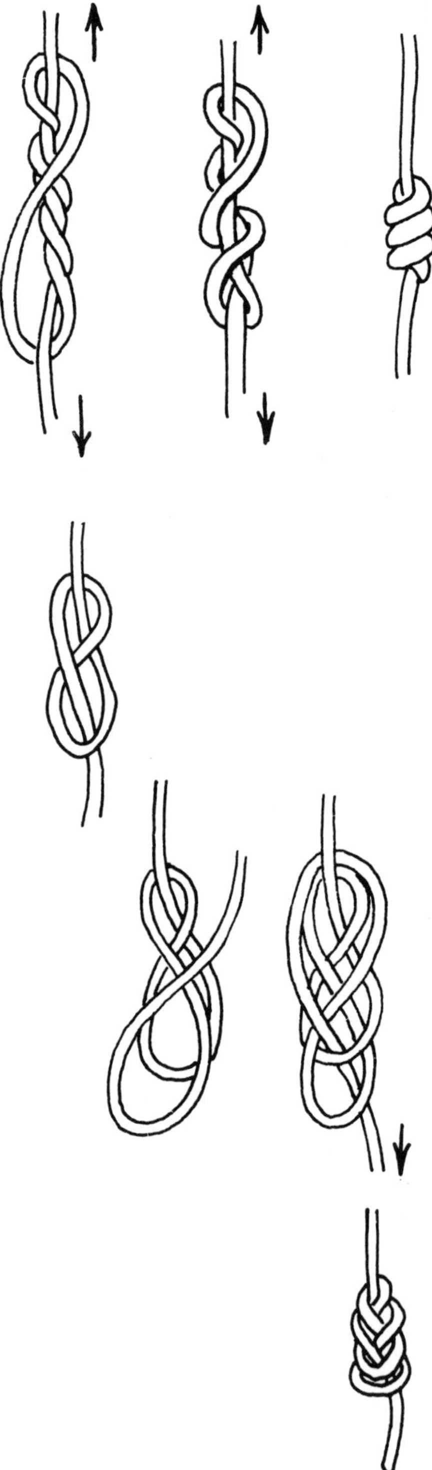

Finishing

Fringe is the most obvious way to finish a macrame piece. There are many types of fringe which can be tied, most of which you can discover easily on your own. Diagram 37 depicts a few knots and fringes we have found useful.

There are also many ways to end a piece without fringe. The simplest way is to end with a row of square knots or clove hitches, wet the knots with glue, varnish, or plastic and trim the cords off flush with the knot. Cords may also be turned up and woven back into a densely knotted pattern. Flat or three-dimensional hangings can be ended by hiding the cord ends in a wooden bar or rod (Diagram 38). If a three-dimensional piece such as a lamp is gradually tapered until only a few cords remain, the ends may be tucked back into the center of the final portion of the piece. Since our usual approach to a problem is to circumvent it, we often begin a fringeless piece at the bottom, or at both ends, taking the cord ends out at the top or the middle of the piece where they are easier to hide (Diagram 39).

38. Cord ends hidden by burying them in a stick used at the top or bottom of the piece.

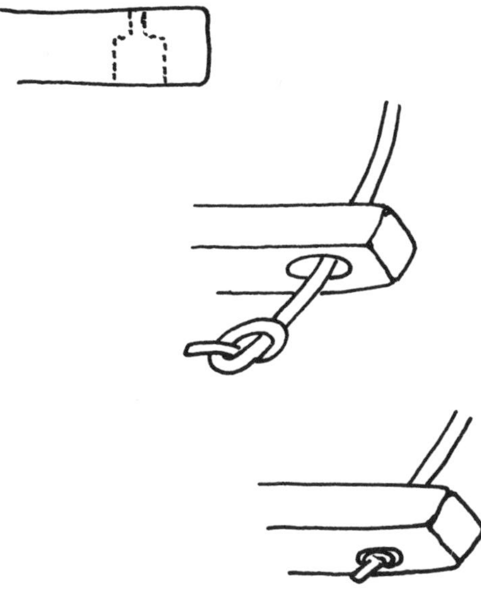

39. Ending in the middle. In the piece shown, the upper and lower parts are tied separately and then joined with ordinary square knots as shown in the drawing at the end. The cords are then trimmed short and pushed to the inside of the piece.

Wrapping

Ropes, cords, fibers, or any other substance may be wrapped with string as a decoration or as means to group the cords in a design. The simplest wrap is a spiral of cord passing around the material. It is the means used to wrap the ends of rope to prevent unraveling and is started and stopped as shown in Diagram 40.

The overhand knot is also used in a simple wrap by being tied repeatedly (Diagram 41). This knot will tend to spiral naturally as it is tied (see left-hand drawing in Diagram 41), but it may be forced to run straight by pulling tightly on the cord as the knot is tied (right-hand drawing, Diagram 41).

Another simple wrap is a reversing hitch which may be tied with a single cord or many cords (Diagram 42). If you are interested in other forms of hitching or wrapping, check knotting encyclopedias under fender hitching or coxcombing.

40. Wrapping (whipping) a rope end to prevent unraveling.

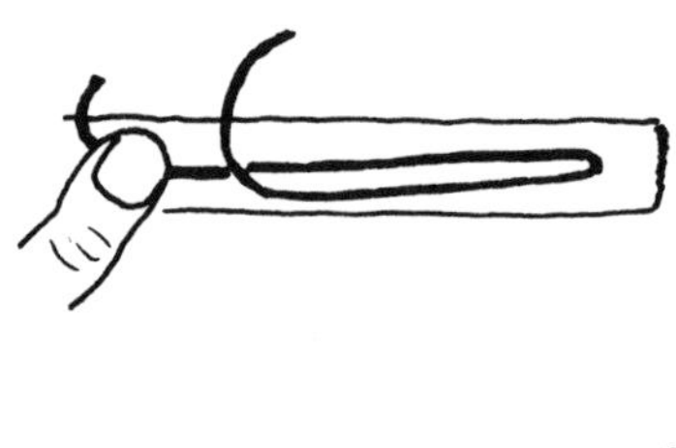

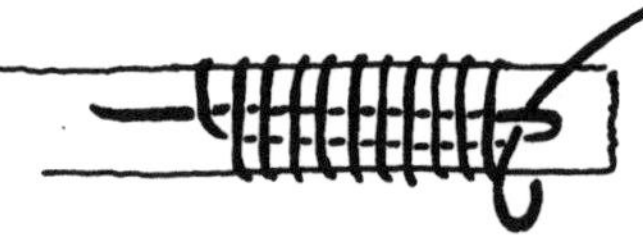

41. The overhand wrap knot may be allowed to spiral (left) or may be pulled into a straight line (right).

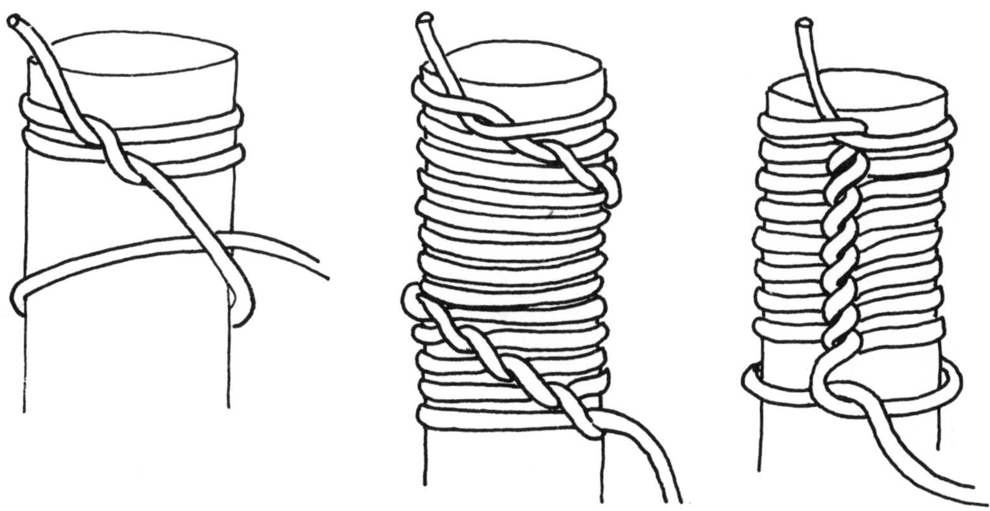

42. Wrapping with a reversing cord (coxcombing). This wrapping may be done with a single cord or with multiple cords. A ridge is formed where the cord reverses, and there will be one ridge for each cord used. One cord produces a single ridge, four cords produce four ridges, and so on.

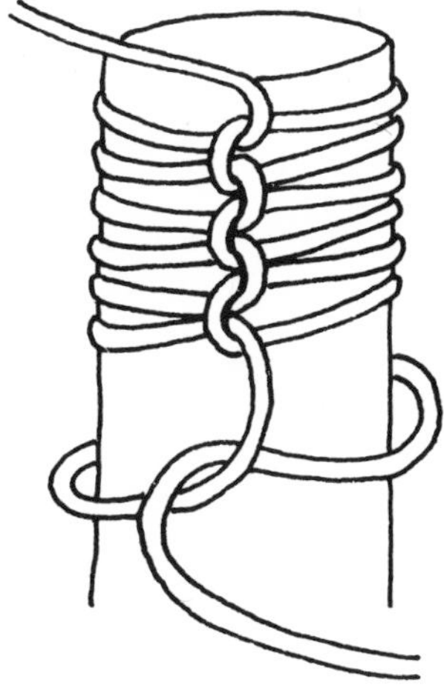

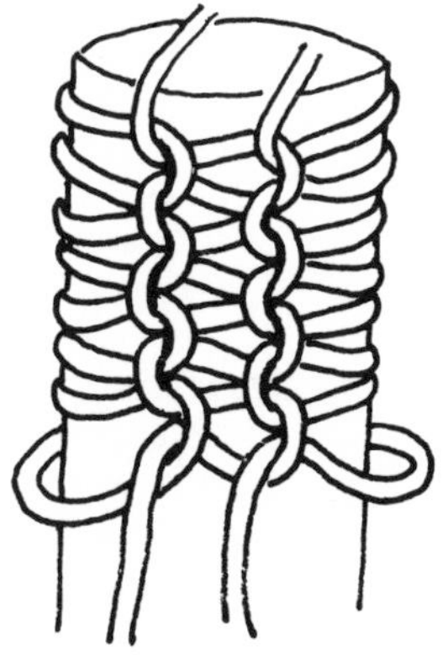

PHOTO SERIES B

Overhand knot wrapping.

1 to 6. Spiral wrap.

7 and 8. Straightening the spiral by pulling on the cord.

1 2

3 4

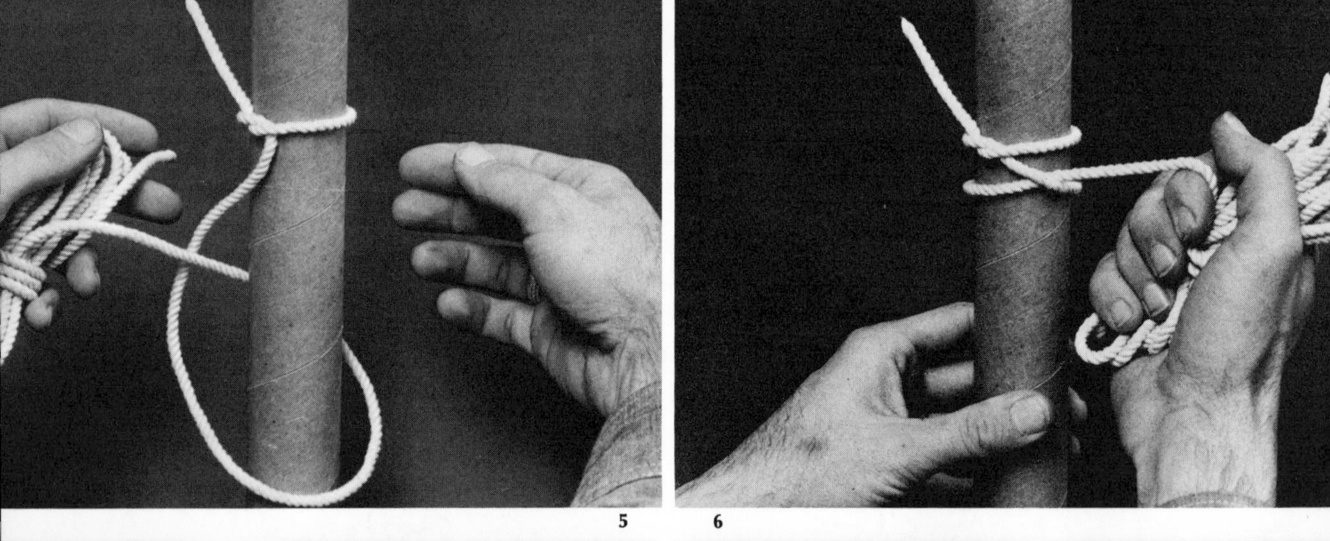

5 6

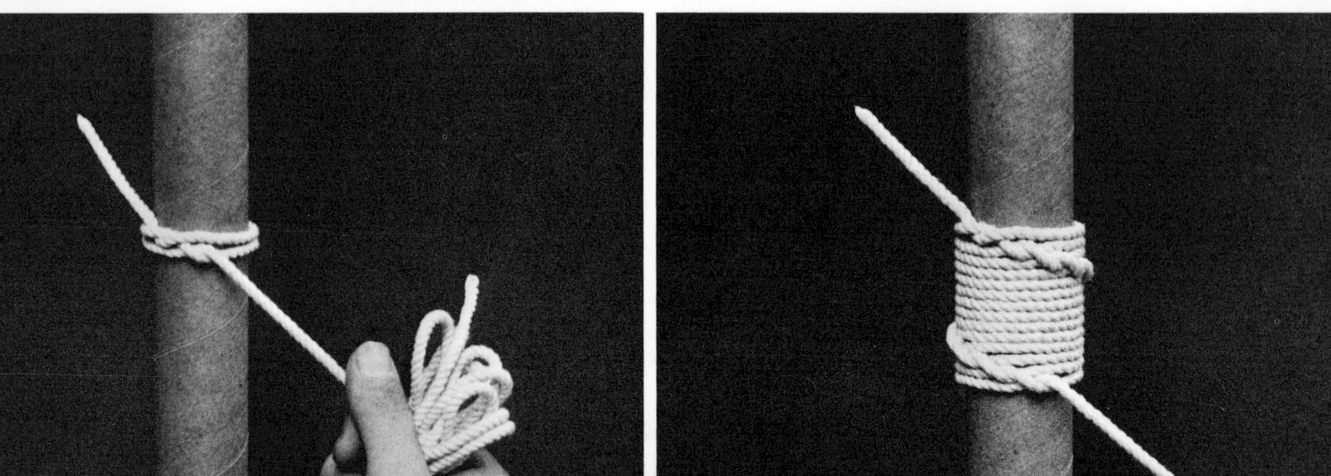

7

8

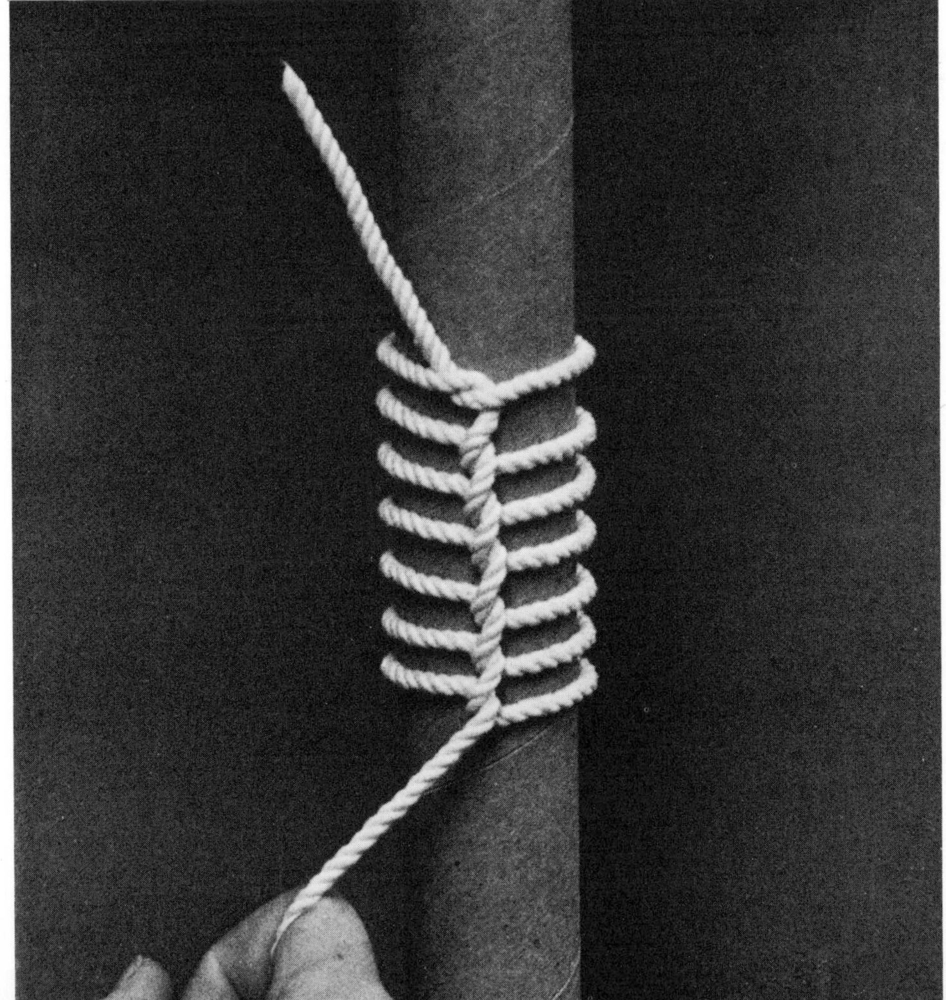

PHOTO SERIES C

1 to 5. Simple coxcombing with a single strand.

6. Coxcombing with 2 strands.

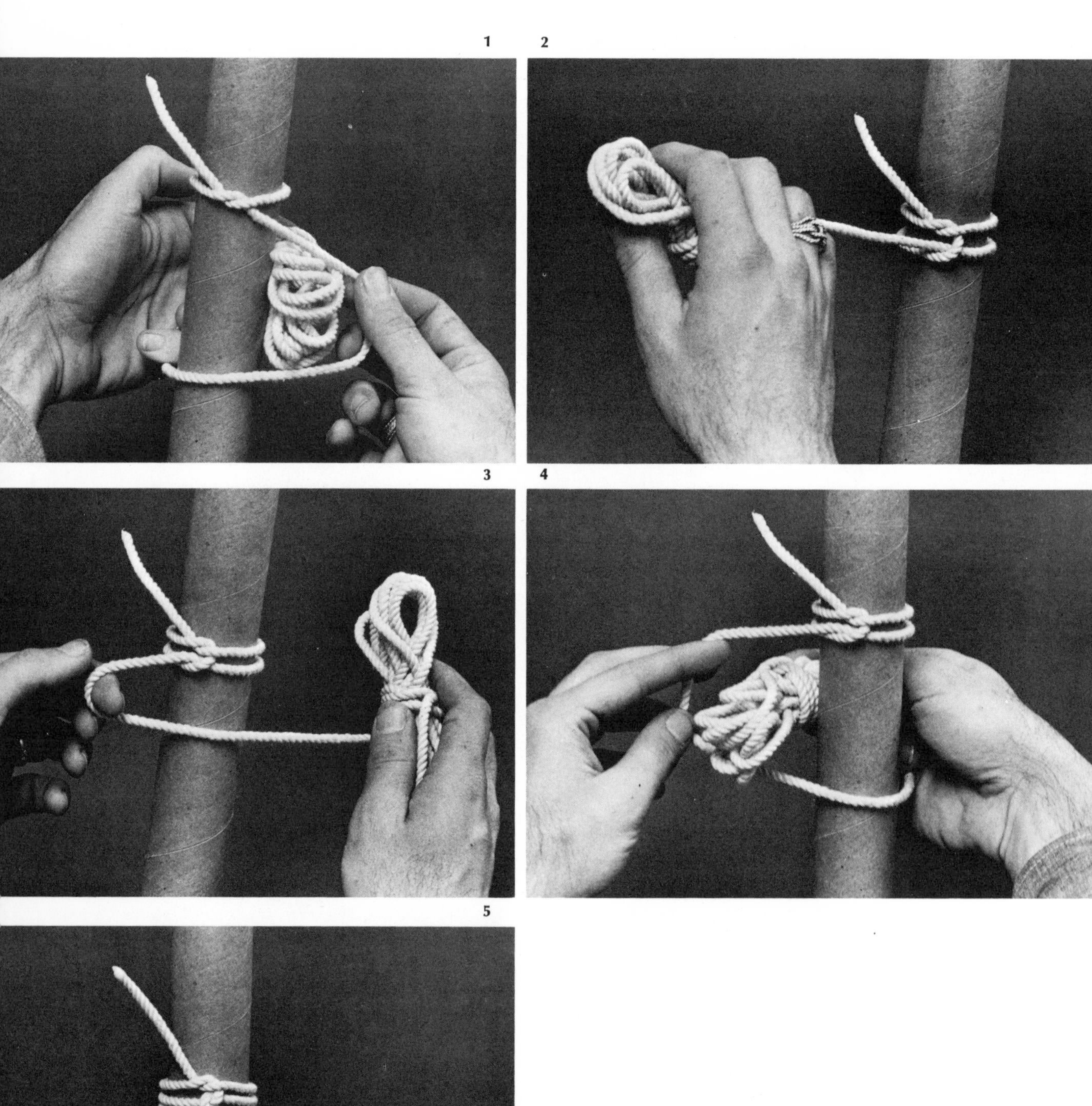

6

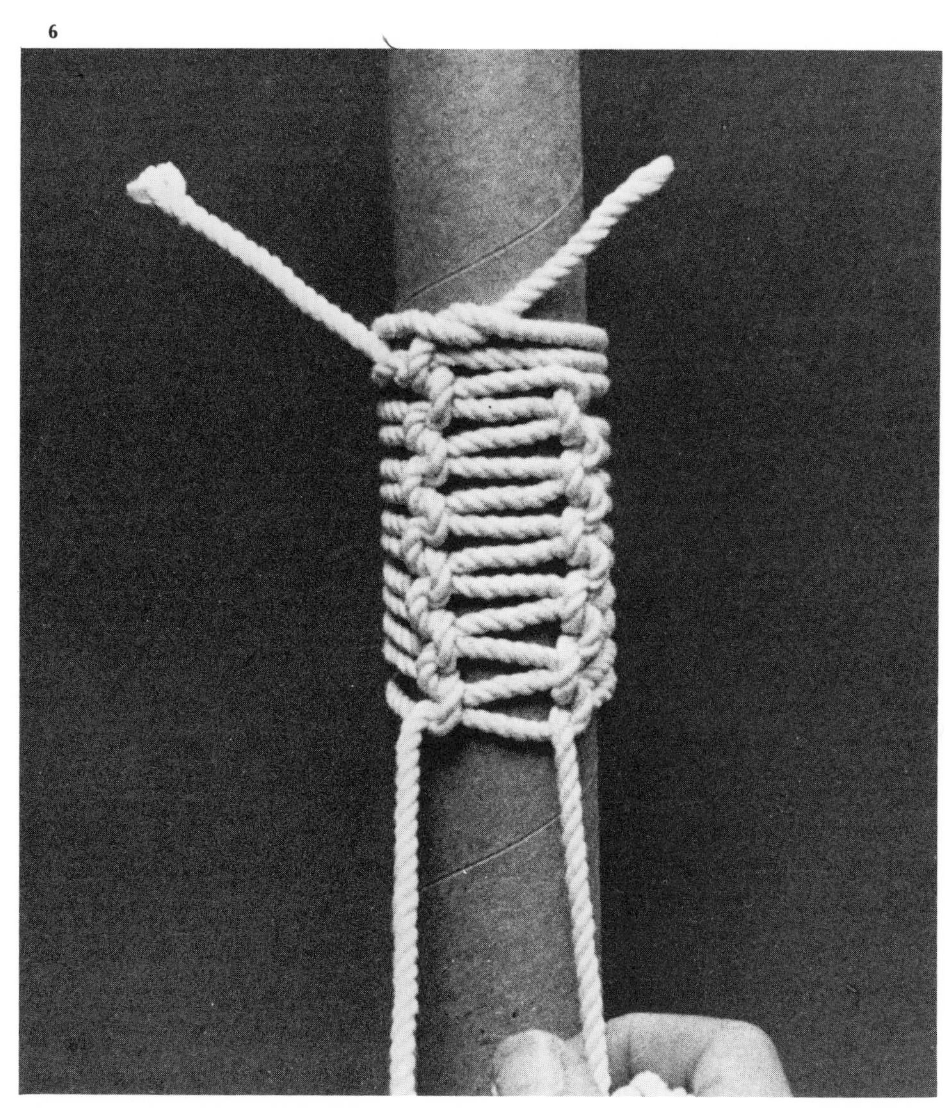

Tassel-Making

Tassels usually consist of bunches of very fine cord or fringe tied onto a larger rope or cord with the point of junction covered by decorative knots or fancy work. The fine cord may be attached to the heavy cord by several means, two of which are shown in Diagram 43. After the fine cords are attached, the area is wrapped with thread and glued to form a pleasing shape (Diagram 44). This wrapping forms the skeleton of the tassel body and is glued or varnished so it will hold its shape. Instead of cord, you could use wood or soft plastic, such as polystyrene, for this layer. Whatever you use, coat it with glue or varnish to smooth the surface for the final wrapping. The finished layer should be made with fine thread carefully wrapped from top to bottom without overlapping. If you have glued or varnished the under layer, wrap the surface layer while the glue or varnish is still slightly tacky, so the thread will stick to it. After the final wrap has been completed, the tassel body is trimmed with turk's heads, sewing notions, beads, pearls, or the like. (See Diagram 45.)

43. Attaching fine tassel cord to the heavier rope when starting to make a tassel.

44. Wrap the base of the tassel to form a decorative shape.

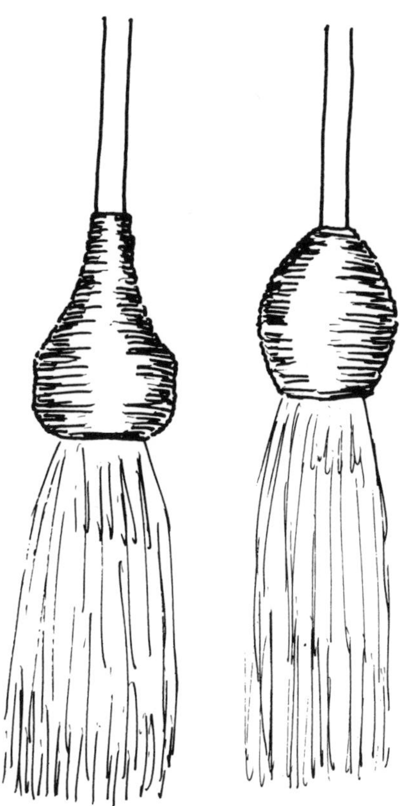

45. Finish the tassel by ornamenting with sewing notions or fine knotting.

SOME EXAMPLES

These lamps are presented not as projects for you to copy nor as particularly fine examples of what you can do with string, but only as a means to show you how some of the principles already discussed are combined in a specific work. Most of what happens in the lamps was improvised as the work progressed. What a knotter should learn is a basic assortment of techniques which can be adapted to solving various problems. You should develop your own skills and seek to create your own designs. Skill in knotting is developed with time and practice; in time, the designs will evolve from your work, each piece presenting new problems and suggesting new works.

Example 1

The first piece was tied as a lampshade for a floor lamp, but it could easily be adapted to a hanging lamp by bolting a socket or globe onto the center hub of the shade holder which forms its skeleton. It was tied with Lily's Macra-Cord, which has enough body to provide the shape shown without any other supporting framework. The shape was created only by the addition and deletion of cord.

Figure 7. A simple knotted lampshade, its shape determined by the addition and deletion of cord. (See also C-3 in the color section.)

Figure 8. A similar lampshade made without decreases in the lower part. Macra-Cord in turquoise, black, and light blue.

Figure 9. Detail of lampshade showing the decreases made in the eggshell and oatmeal cord.

46.

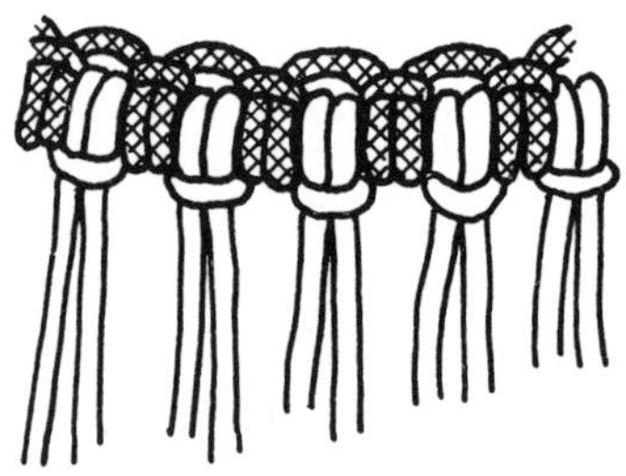

47.

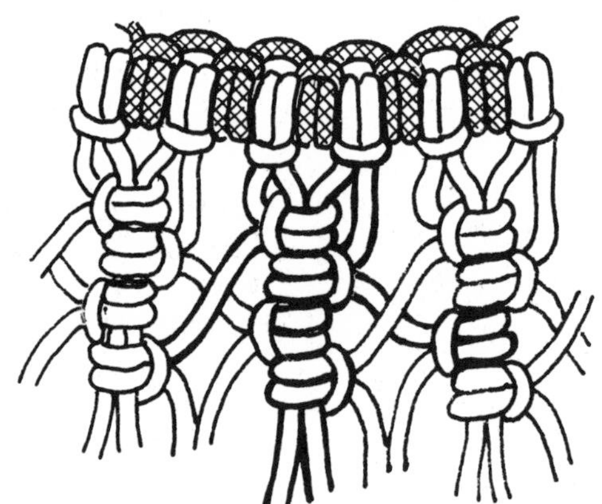

Three colors were used: 66 eggshell, 66 orange, and 45 oatmeal, all in 14-foot lengths (7 seven-foot working lengths). Sixty-six doubled cords of eggshell are fastened to the rim, using lark's head knots with an oatmeal spacer cord, as shown in Diagram 46.

The first two inches are tied in the alternating lark's head pattern shown in Diagram 47. As this pattern is tied, the shade will decrease in diameter below the rim. After tying the pattern, switch to the alternating square knot pattern, which will be used for the rest of the lamp. This pattern is probably the best for a piece like this in which a dense self-supporting pattern is desired. Tie the pattern tightly with the knots close together as shown in Diagram 48. After two rows of alternating square knots, the first increase is made. Eleven increases are made—every three square knots as indicated in Diagram 49. A single cord is doubled through the loops of the preceding row of square knots and used to tie a Japanese crown knot, as shown in Diagram 50.

48.

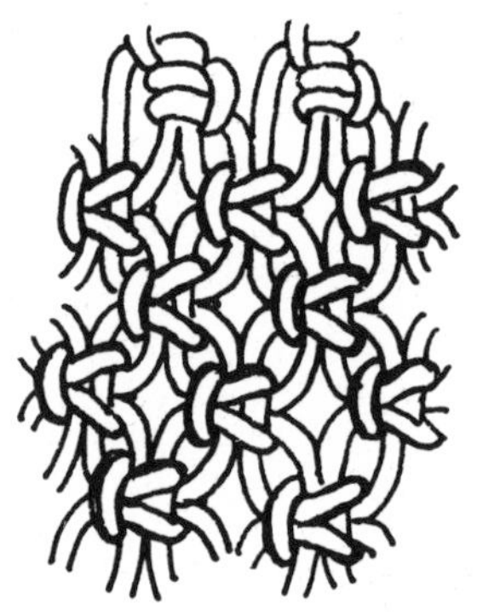

49. Arrows show where to increase.

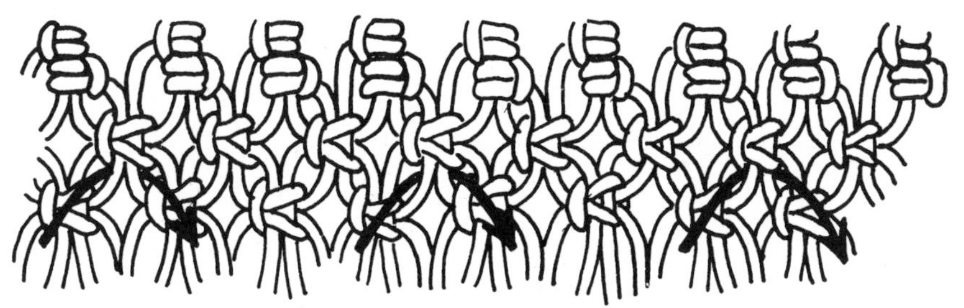

50. Tying the Japanese crown knot in the hand (left) and on a knotted piece (right).

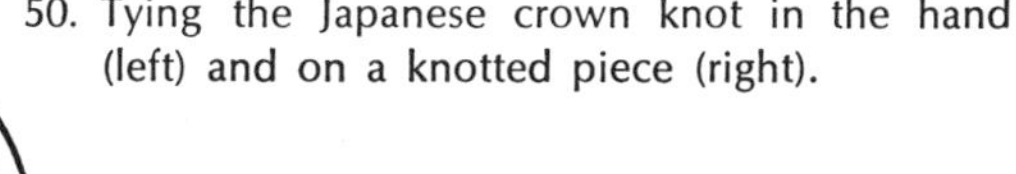

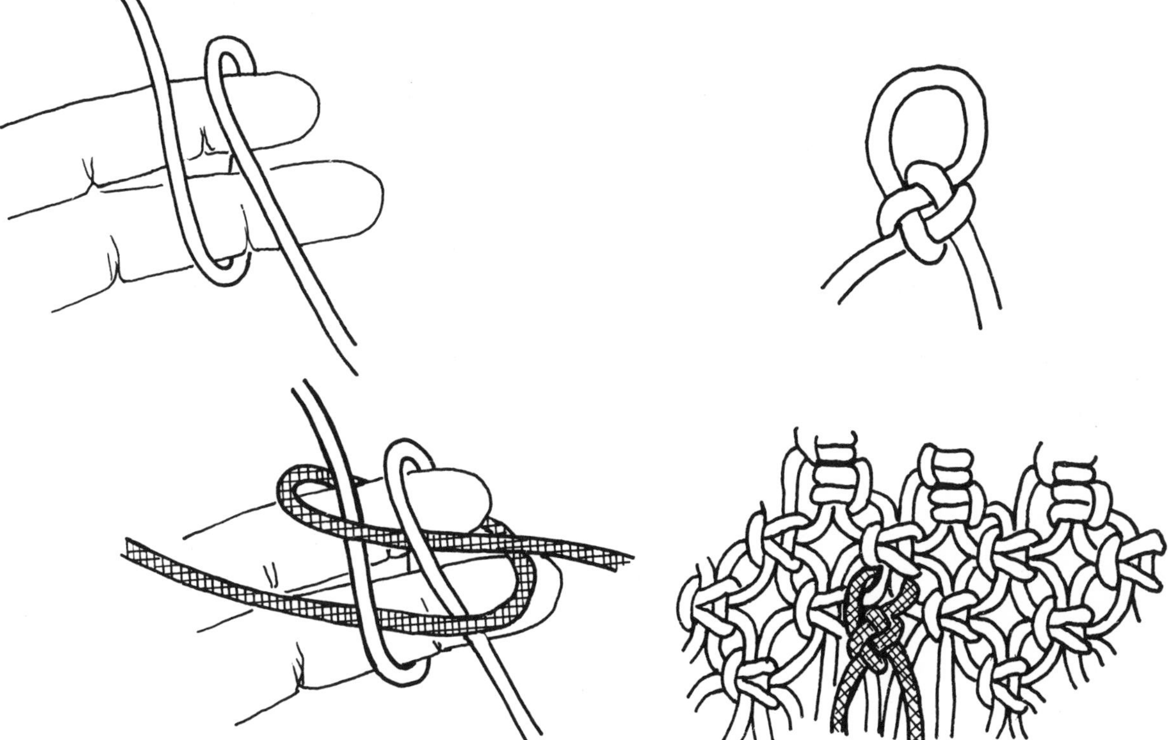

51.

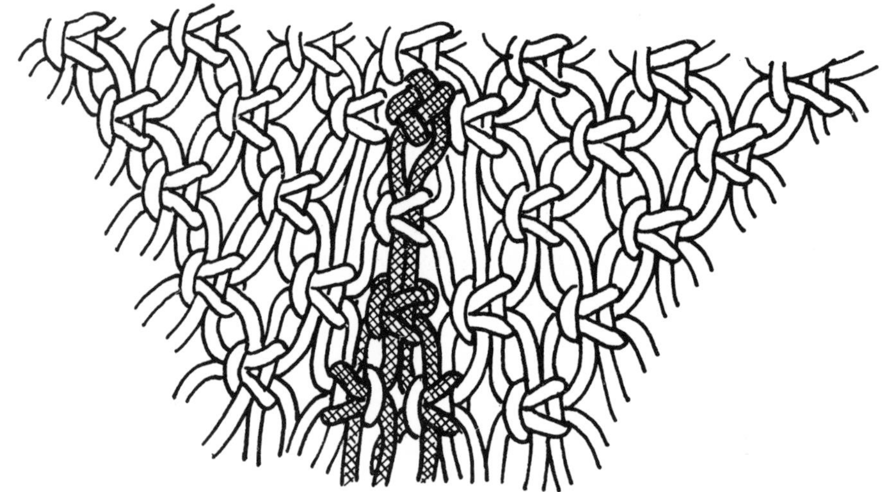

Then two rows of alternating square knots are tied, handling the added cord as shown in Diagram 51, and a second oatmeal cord is added to the first in the usual fashion (Diagram 51). After two more rows of alternating square knots, a set of four cords is added in the line of increases previously made (Diagram 52). These cords are incorporated into the alternating square knot pattern, which is continued for four more rows. Four orange cords are added in each area, then two rows of square knots, then another addition of orange cords, to complete the increases. There are now 308 working cords.

By tying nine rows of square knots with no further changes, you can get the upper portion of the lamp to continue its curve out and down. At this point, the lamp could be continued down for a few inches and finished in fringe, for a lampshade shaped like the drawing in Diagram 53 or the shade pictured on page 70. In this example, however, the number of working cords was decreased to bring the shade in and then down. The decreases could have been made in the orange areas, but we wanted the orange to continue while the eggshell cord gradually decreased to a point and vanished. If the decreases had been made in the orange areas, the lamp would have looked like the drawing in Diagram 54. We wanted to decrease the eggshell cord rapidly, but if we had done so without increasing slightly in the orange areas, the shade would have tapered abruptly inward. To soften the tapering of the lamp, we deleted in the center of the eggshell cords, at the same time adding cord in the orange areas. By decreasing more than we increased, the lamp was made to taper gradually.

After the nine rows of square knots are tied above, make an increase of four more orange cords as before, but at the same time, delete four eggshell cords in the middle of the eggshell area. Make no further increases, but continue to delete four eggshell cords every other row until the eggshell cord has been completely removed from the shade.

Continue knotting in the square knot pattern, deleting the oatmeal-colored cords in the same way as the eggshell cords until only the orange cords remain.

Tie eight or nine rows of square knots with the orange cord, finishing in a scalloped edge. The border may be left fringed or the cords overhand-knotted, glued, and trimmed short as shown.

52.

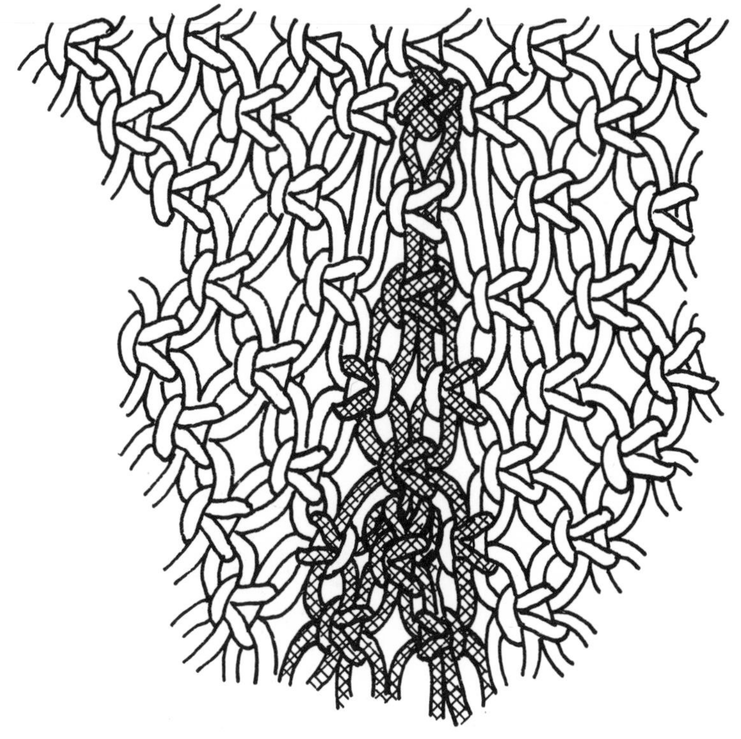

53.

54.

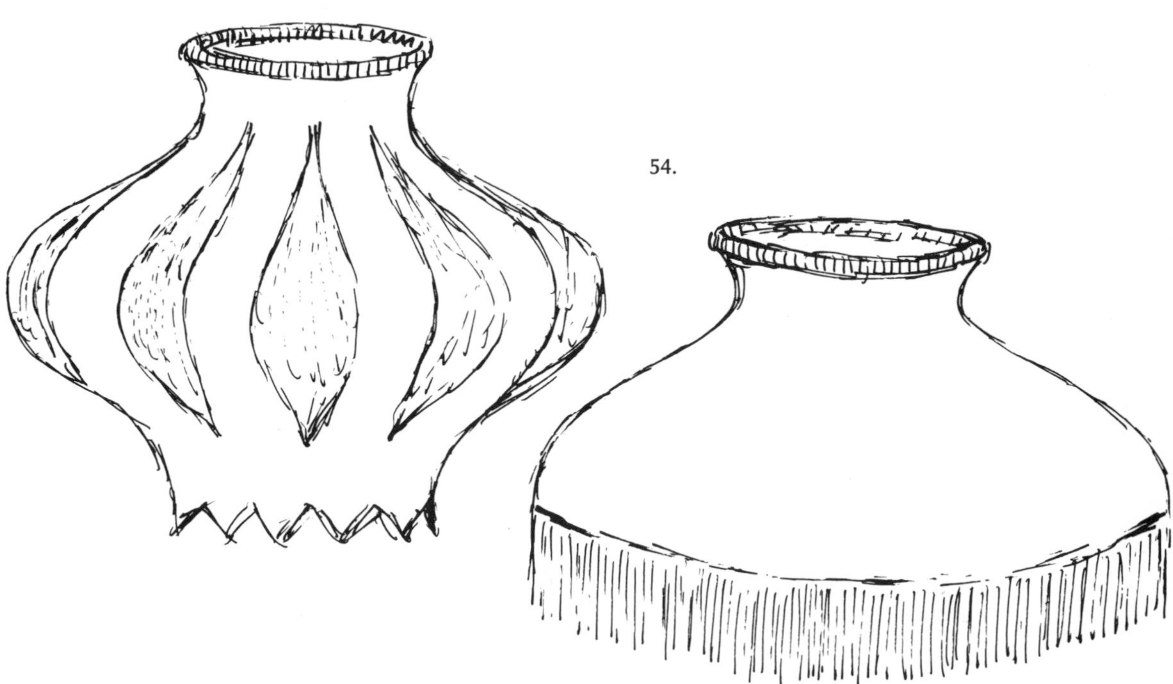

Example 2

The frame parts for this lamp are readily available brass rings and lampshade holders, which are knotted into the project as it is tied, beginning from the bottom and knotting upward. (Use two 2¼″ brass rings; one 3½″ brass ring; and two 8″ lampshade holders.)

The shape of this lamp is supported and determined by the circular support members. Again, we used Lily Mill's Co. Macra-Cord, which has sufficient body to permit modification of the basic circular shape without other supports. Most other cord would be too soft to use in this type of lamp, but could be varnished or glued to hold the shape.

Figure 10. View of the finished lamp as tied.

Figure 11. Detail of the lamp showing the knotting in the lower portion.

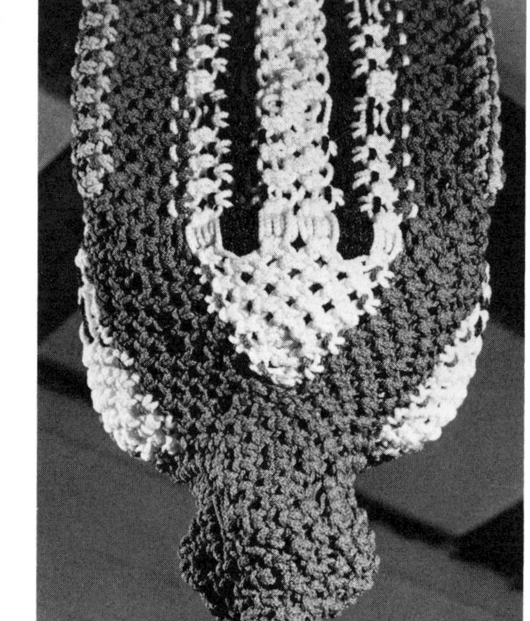

Figure 12. The finished lamp as hung—upside down.

Figure 13. Adding a split D-ring by bending it open, inserting it into the knotting, and then bending it closed with pliers.

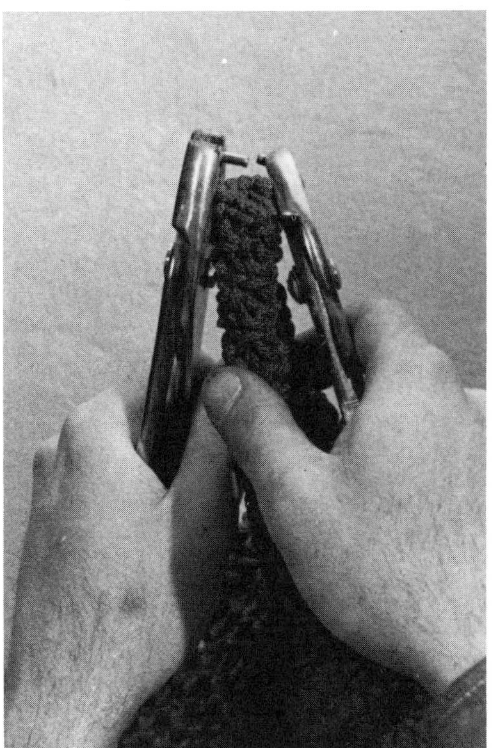

55.

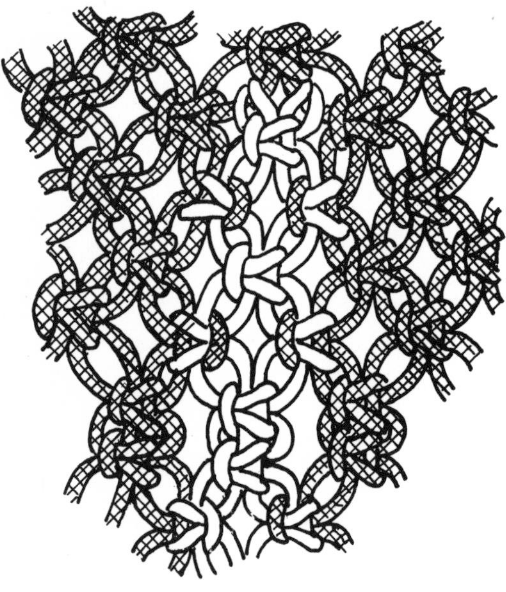

56. Tying a ring into a piece with square knots.

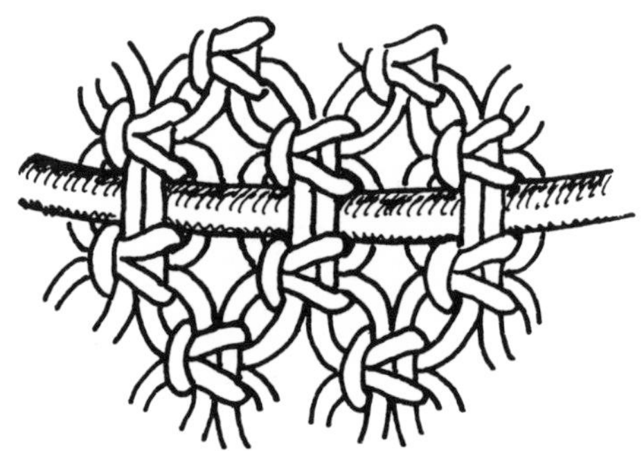

The lamp is started on a 2¼″ ring with 16 black cords. In order to cover the ring and space the cords, a spacer cord is used with the ends hidden, as shown earlier in Diagram 46.

After two rows of alternating square knots, the first addition of cord is made. In the lamp that is illustrated, the added cords are of a contrasting color (white). They are added four at a time by the method described earlier, the 4 sets spaced equally around the hanging. With the 48 working cords, tie 4 rows of the alternating square knot pattern, followed by a row of double square knots, then add 4 more groups of white cord in line with the first addition (see Diagram 55). Tie three rows of alternating square knots with the 64 working cords, then add the 3½″ ring into the lamp. Any of the methods described above may be used to tie the ring into the pattern; Ellen used square knots (Diagram 56).

Tie two rows of alternating square knots below the ring, and delete 4 sets of 4 cords from the black area. Tie one row of square knots and delete the rest of the black cord in the usual way.

57. Tying a ring into a piece with clove hitches.

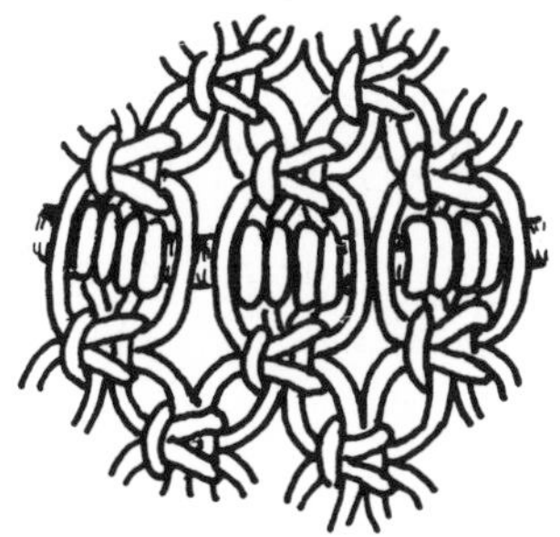

58. Working the corner edges. A cord is added to the piece by attaching it to the rim with a lark's head and then tying it into the knotting as shown.

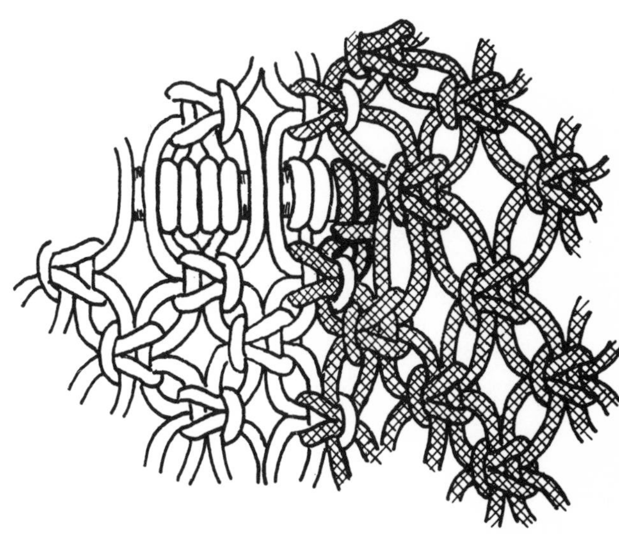

Now only the white cords remain in the working pattern. Carry the black cords along inside the lamp as you work, tying two rows of alternating square knots with the white and adding the second 2¼″ ring. In this case, the ring is too small to clove hitch all the cords over, so it was tied in by clove hitching only the two center cords (Diagram 57).

Below this ring, the lamp expands outward rapidly to reach the diameter of the shade holder. Tie one row of square knots below the ring with white cord and begin adding the black cords back into the pattern. The black cord could be added in any of the ways we discussed before, but in this case, Ellen chose to add it two cords at a time in 8 areas around the pattern instead of 4 as earlier. Thus, 8 black stripes appear in the white and are carried through the pattern by making a second addition of black cords two rows below the first. The black cords used for the stripes are the same ones deleted before and no new black cord is added.

At this point, 4 "corners" are created by the rapid addition of four sets of 4 cords at four points around the lamp. Ellen used turquoise cord for the corners.

Adding cord rapidly in straight lines increases the diameter of the piece but at the same time causes it to become roughly square in shape. To keep such a hanging round while increasing it, the increases should be made at more than 4 places and at a slower rate.

The entire hanging is continued down in the alternating square knot pattern for 8 rows before tying in the upper shade holder.

Only the black and white cords are tied over the shade holder; the blue cords continue in the alternating square knot pattern outside the rim of the holder. Tie the cords over the rim as you tied the last ring. At each edge of each corner, tie a blue cord to the rim with the lark's head and add it to the alternating square knot pattern of the blue cords (Diagram 58). Tie two rows of alternating square knots with all cords below the rim, securely locking the rim into the knotted pattern.

59. Working the corners. Four dark cords are tied behind the knotting as shown in the second and third drawings. This maneuver causes the corners to pucker outward and "squares" the piece.

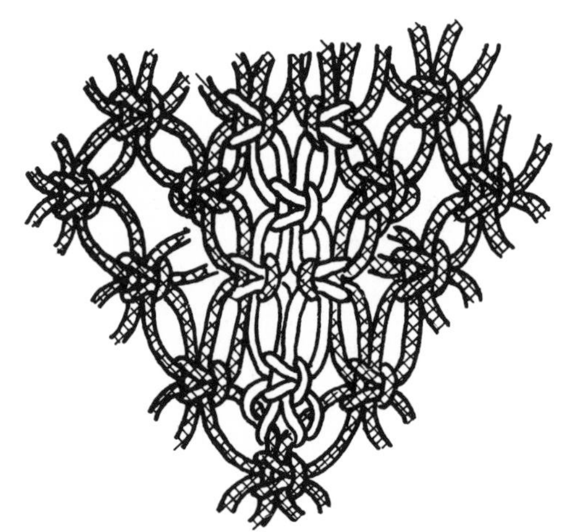

Add four light blue cords at each corner in the usual fashion, and continue working down in the alternating square knot pattern, modifying the pattern at the corners as shown in Diagram 59.

The four side panels are tied in any pattern which will allow your hands to reach inside to wire the lamp later. This part of the lamp should be about 8 or 9 inches long. About one inch above the lower lampshade holder, delete the light blue cords from the pattern. After two rows of square knots, tie the black and white cords over the lower rim, continuing the dark blue past the rim for three rows, making two decreases in the dark blue in the usual fashion. Reconnect the white and blue below the rim and tie 3 rows of alternating square knots with blue and white only, thus removing black from the pattern. Delete 4 white cords in each area along the edges, at the same time replacing the deleted white cords with blue cords earlier removed from the corners. The blue area should look from the rim down the way it does in Diagram 60. Tie two rows of alternating square knots, then delete 4 sets of 4 white cords from each panel in the next 3 rows, eliminating white from the pattern as

60 and 61. Decreasing in the lower part of the lamp. The cords are deleted four at a time in the usual manner.

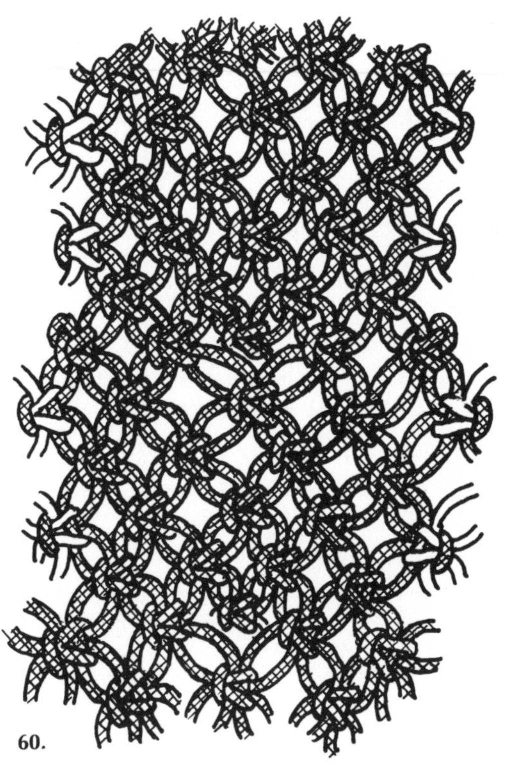

60.

the blue continues down, as shown in Diagram 61.

Make one final decrease in the blue and knot 3 rows of alternating square knots with the remaining blue cords. The blue cords removed above may be added back into the pattern briefly to produce a slight bulb shape, and the pattern rapidly tapered to produce a shape like the one in the lamp pictured.

The deleted cords hanging inside the lamp are trimmed and a narrow tube knotted down for a length of 8 to 10 inches, decreasing to 12 cords and then to 8. To finish, the ends are square knotted together and stuffed back up into the hollow tube formed by the knotting.

We liked this lamp better upside down, so we hang it that way.

This project sounds very complex when described in detail, but it is really easy to execute. With no plan to confuse her, Ellen combined the techniques described earlier to produce the desired final form. When working on such a project, the knotter should not be concerned with the complexity of the finished piece, but should concentrate on solving the many small problems as they arise.

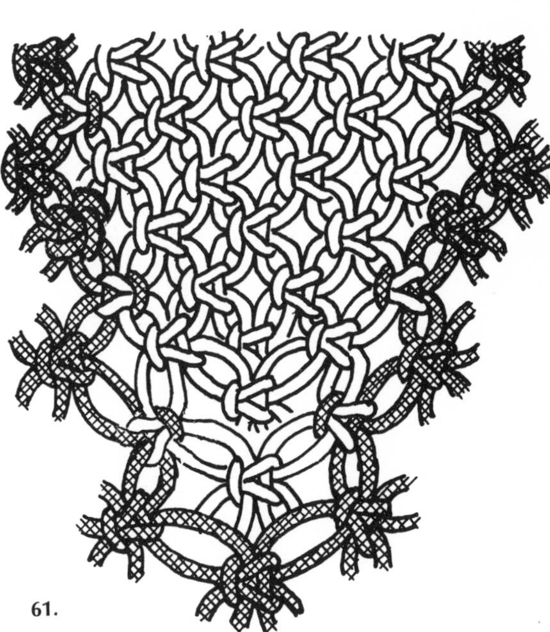

61.

Example 3

Here's a lamp with no frame members at all. You could make this shape with rings and hoops if you wanted to, but if the string used has a fair amount of body it will hold its shape without them. The lamp shown was made with Macra-Cord. This (Diagram 62) is one way to start a project without hitching the cords over a ring or a stick.

This lamp also has a bulb shape at its upper end, but without rings to support it. After the knotting is worked outward and inward to form the bulb, the first cords added below are looped through the upper part of the lamp before being tied into the pattern. These cords support the upper part of the lamp against the downward pull of the weight of the rest of the lamp (see Diagram 63).

Flare the lower part of the lamp outward by adding cords until the desired maximum diameter is reached. Work in a tightly knotted pattern like the one shown, so the lamp will be rigid and hold its shape. After reaching the desired width, tie four or six rows of a rigid pattern and end the lamp in fringe or any way you like.

62. Starting a lamp without framework. The starting pattern is the same as that shown in the second drawing of Diagram 23, with the cord used to hang the piece threaded through the center of the knotting.

63. The black cord shown in the diagram is used to hold the shape of the knotting against the weight of the piece.

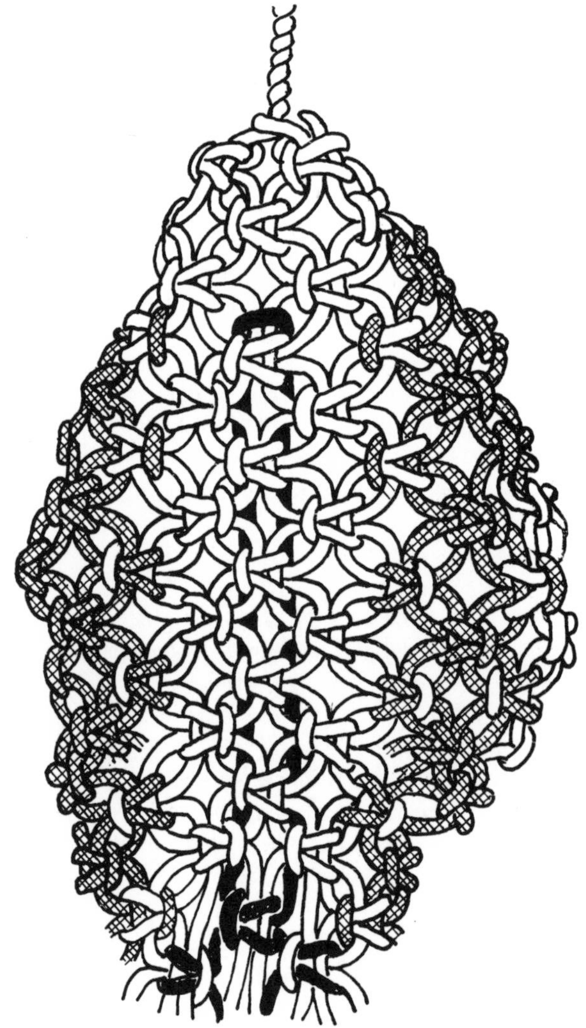

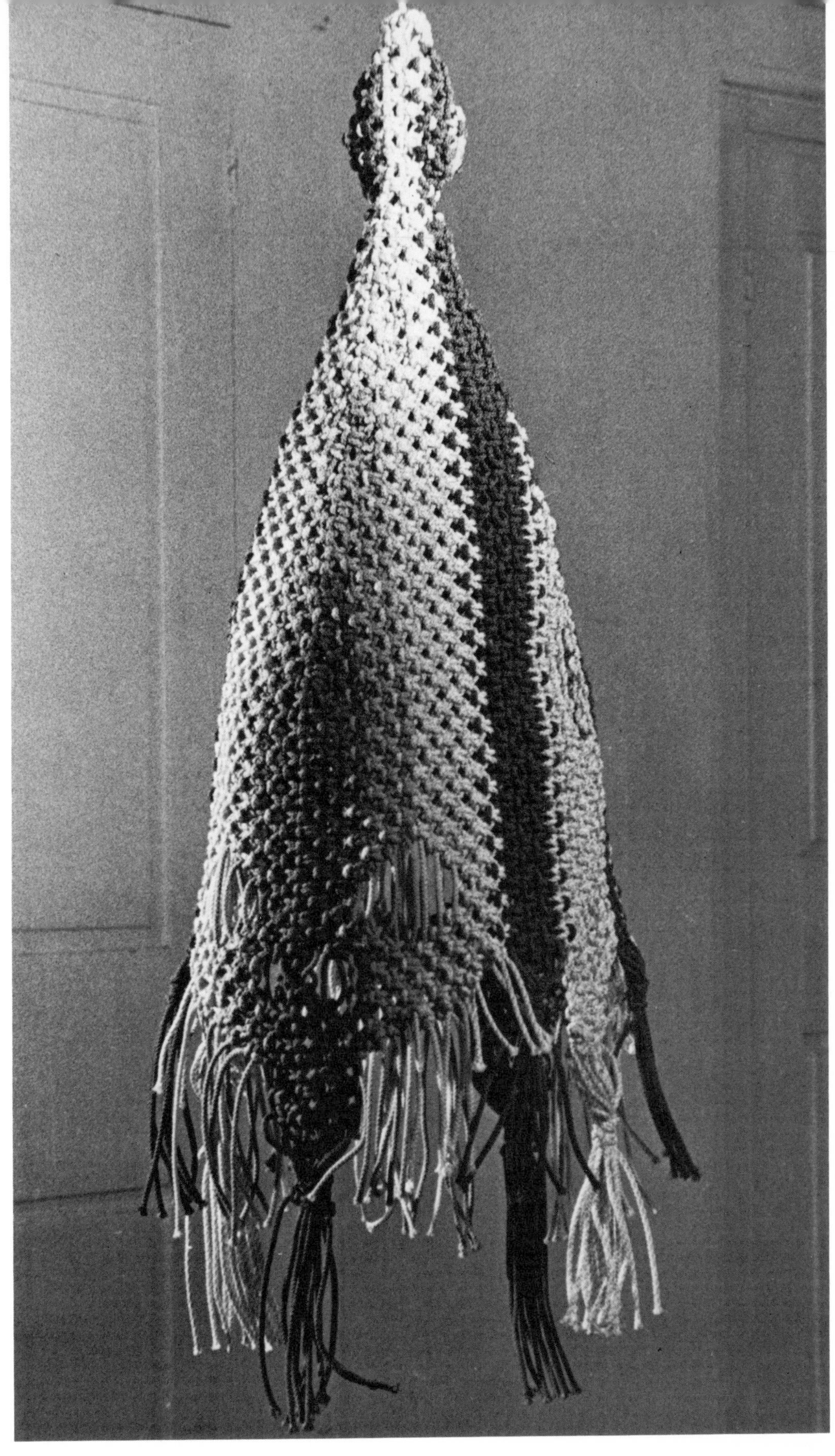

Figure 14. Hanging lamp made without framework. The shape is self-supporting.

64. Tensive (left) and compressive (right) forces tend to deform a knotted piece.

65. Resisting compressive force by use of rigid struts (left) or a rigid hoop (right).

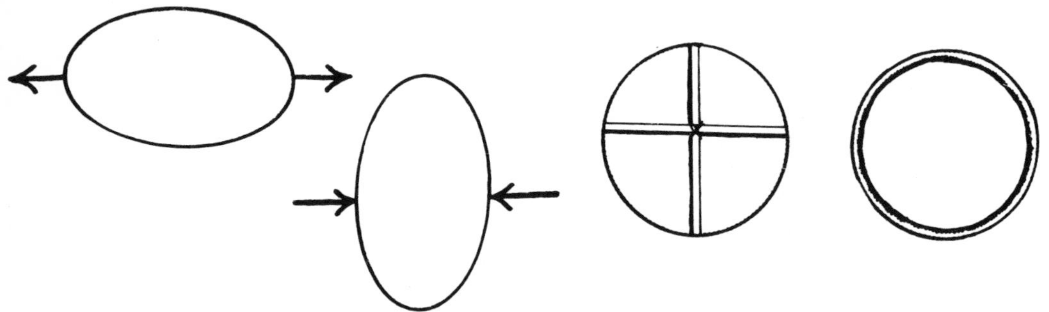

Theoretical Considerations

These lamps illustrate some important concepts in our rather simple-minded approach to engineering. In most of knotting, we are concerned with two types of forces: tensive force and compressive force (see Diagram 64). The tendency of a lamp to collapse inward may be thought of as a compressive force, and the tendency of it to stretch out of shape downward as a tensive force. Compressive force—as in the collapse of a macrame lamp—may be resisted most simply with a rigid frame member like a stick or a metal rim (Diagram 65).

Tension can be resisted by a solid member or by something nonrigid, such as cord or a cable, which is resistant to stretch (Diagram 66).

In most lamps and three-dimensional macrame pieces, both types of force are present and with experience you will learn how and when to use framework in your work in order to counteract them.

66. Resisting tensive force by a wire framework (left) or by use of guy wire cords (right).

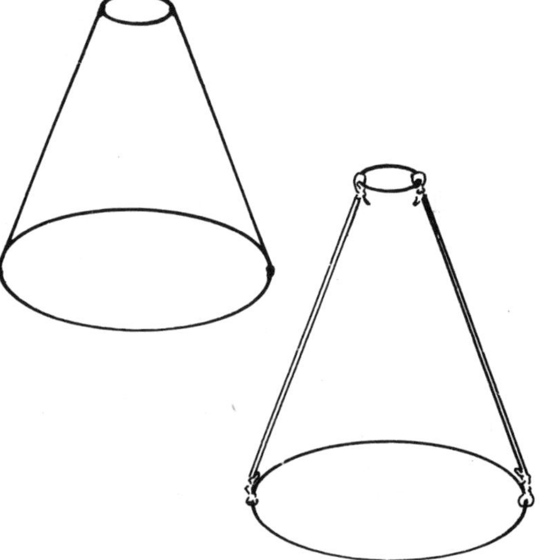

Theoretical Considerations Reconsidered: Cheating

Most of what we have just said about support and framework in macrame design is made inapplicable by resorting to a rather simple trick. If cord is made rigid, it will be self-supporting and no longer require framework or other support. The easiest way to do this is to varnish the cord or thoroughly impregnate it with liquid plastic. For example, if you had a lampshade shaped like the one in Diagram 66A and wanted to make it without rings or hoops or any other support, you could tie it in any cord, even the softest yarn, and treat it to make it rigid after the piece is done. Further information about materials and methods for treating cord are discussed later. We occasionally varnish or plastic-coat cord, but for most purposes we prefer the appearance and texture of untreated cord.

66A.

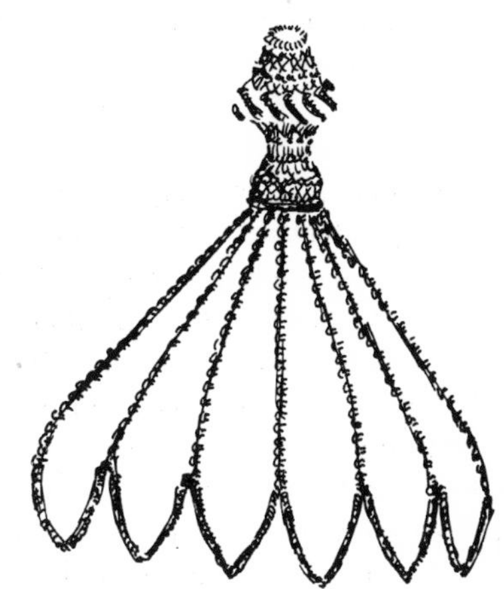

67. Adding cords to a partly finished piece.

Shape

Shapes more complex than those of the lamps described above usually evolve as the piece is tied. Sometimes we keep going down, adding on successive cords to produce a long hanging. Other times we go back and add cord on the part of the hanging already completed to make the piece grow out. When going back to add cord to a piece already knotted, add the cord like this (see Diagram 67).

More complex projects may evolve in several directions at once: out, up, and down. Often, smaller subunits are tied and added to the growing work. We use three basic methods of tying pieces together. The first method results in a seamless joint, and it is used when both pieces can be left partly finished with an "open" edge (Diagram 68). Two pieces with open edges are joined as shown in Diagram 69. When it's not possible to leave both pieces with open edges and one part must be completed before joining, finish the edge as shown in Diagram 70. Leave the other piece with an open edge and join the two (Diagram 71). When both edges must be finished before joining the two parts, finish both as just described and then lace them together with a separate cord (Diagram 72).

68. The right-hand border of this knotting had been left "open" for joining to another piece.

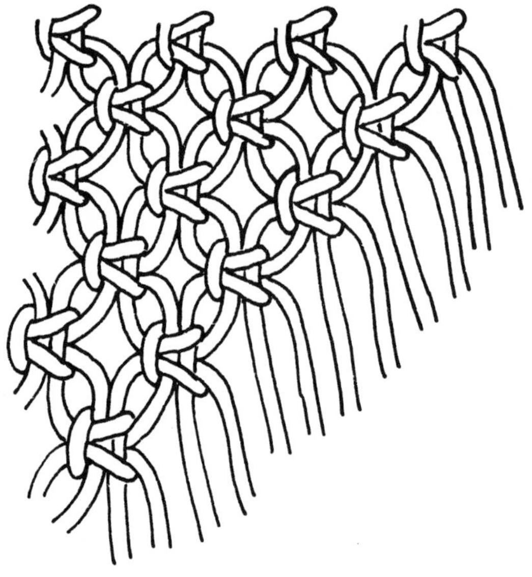

69. Joining two pieces with open edges by square knotting.

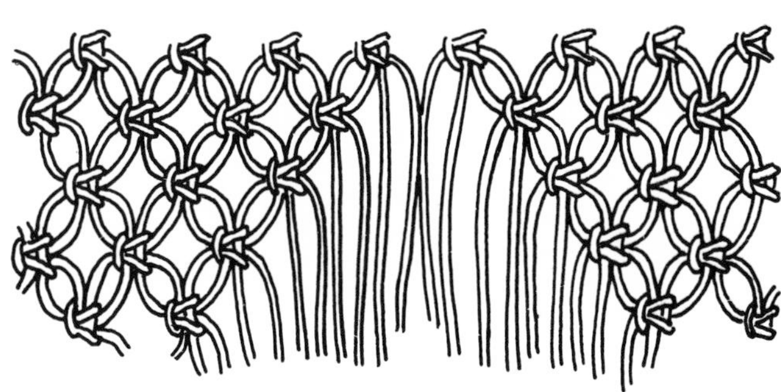

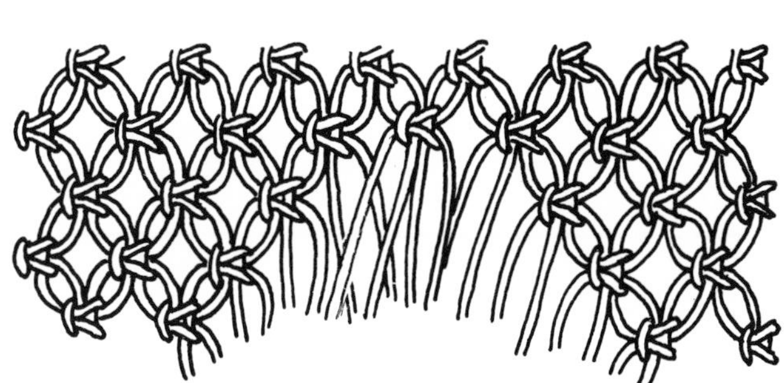

70. A piece with a "closed" edge suitable for joining to another.

71. Joining a piece with a closed edge to one with an open edge. The pieces are joined with lark's head knots as shown.

72. Two pieces with closed edges are simply laced together with a single cord.

Figure 15. Lamp with stained glass panels—18″ diameter. Tied with cotton seine twine No. 30 and No. 120. The glass and lead were salvaged from a demolished church. (See also the color photo, C-6.)

FINISHED PROJECT PICTURES

A.

B.

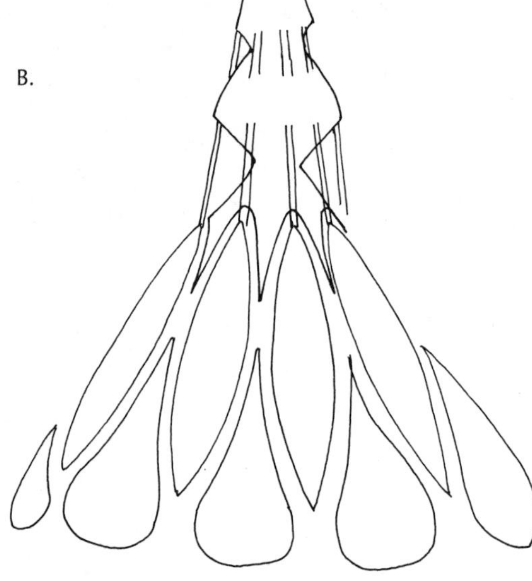

NOTES ON THE LAMP

This lamp (Figure 15) was started by attaching the heavy cords to the framework something like this (Diagram A).

The smaller cords were added by tying square knots over the large cords, gradually adding more small cord until the upper shape was formed. The cords are increased and decreased to form the shape of the lamp (Diagram B). The knotting attaches to the heavy cords as required to maintain the shape desired. The glass panels are leaded and tied to the heavy cords by pressing the cord into the lead channel (see Figures 16 and 17 and Diagram C).

C.

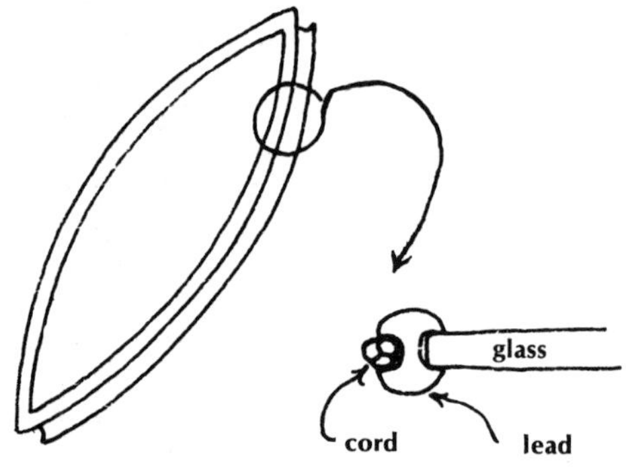

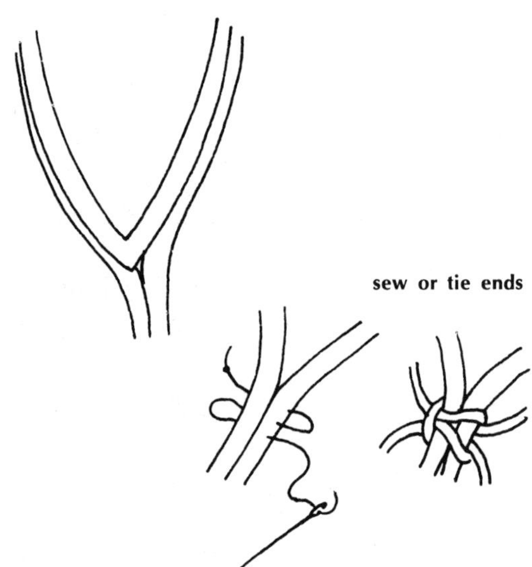

Figures 16 and 17. Details of the lamp showing knotted patterns. Notice that the heavy cords carry the panels and the weight of the bottom rim. The finer cord creates the lacy pattern which attaches to the heavy cord and the lower rim.

16

17

Figure 18. A "quickie" made from short lengths of left-over Macra-Cord. Its use is as yet undetermined.

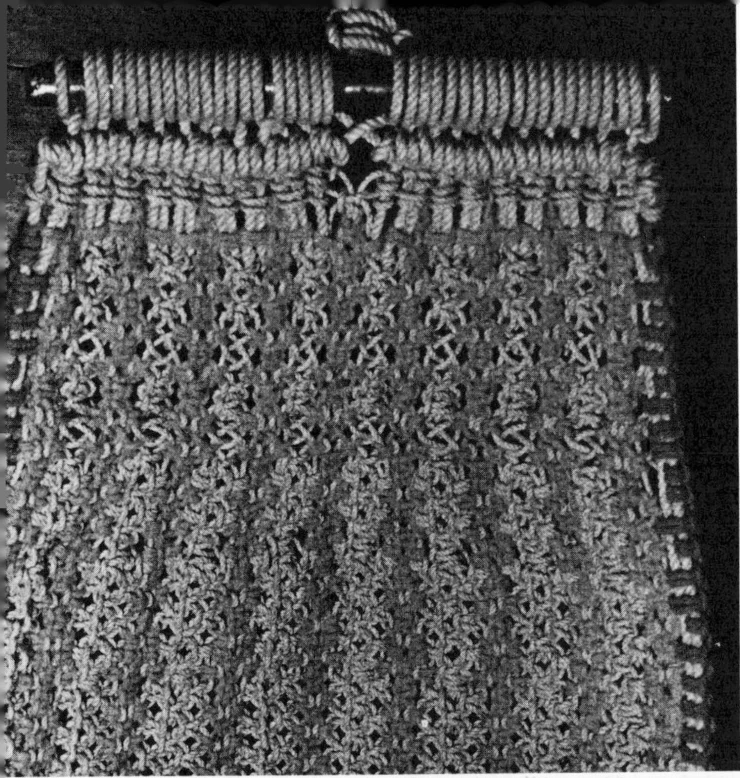

Figure 19. Detail of the cradle shown below.

Figure 20. Macrame baby cradle. Solid brass base with cotton seine twine and acrylic yarn knotting. (See also C-11.)

21.

Figures 21 and 22. Macrame swing in various sizes of cotton seine twine. (See also C-10.) The rim is an iron tire from a broken hay rake wheel found on the farm. Other parts and fittings are bronze marine hardware or home-made from ¼″ diameter steel rod. Large enough to hold two adults comfortably, it was made in about twenty hours of work.

22.

Figure 23. Front door panel covering two window panes. Made from jute and sisal twine bought at a local junk yard.

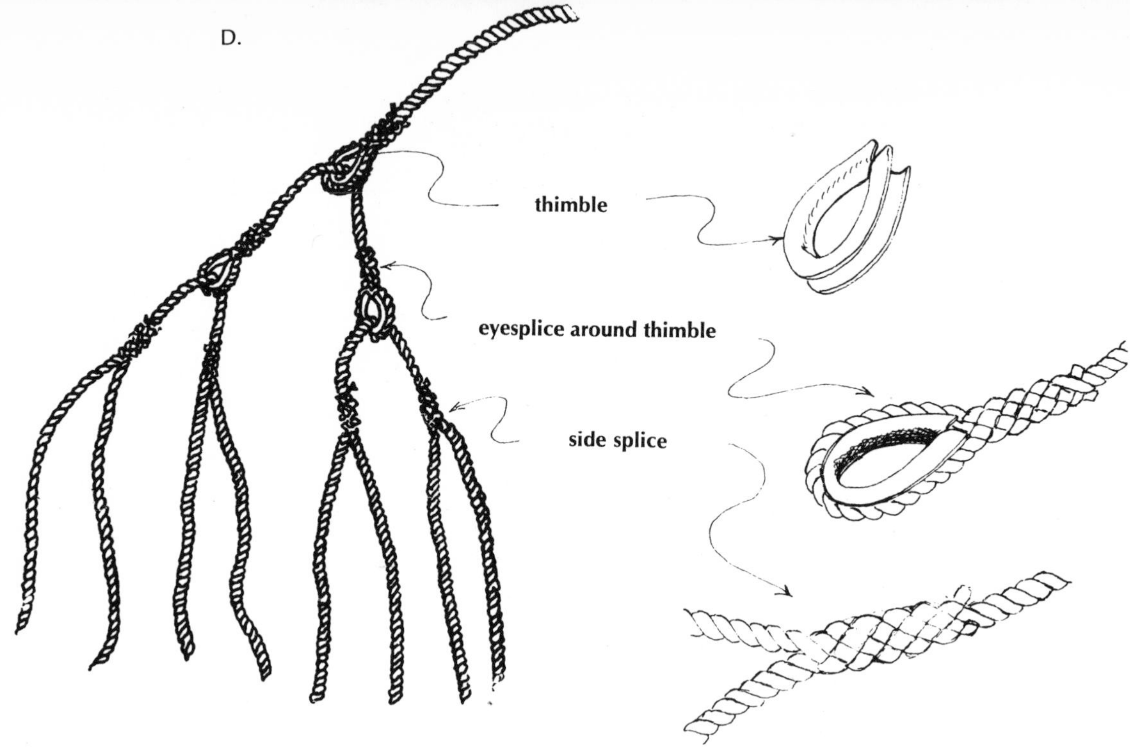

NOTES ON THE SWING

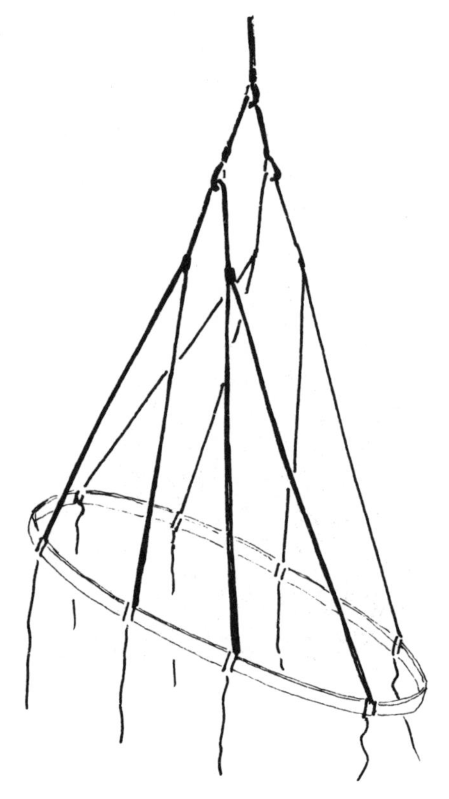

The principle of suspension of the swing is similar to the lamp with the stained glass panels: Heavy cords support the rim carrying the weight of the rim and of the knotted pattern. There are eight ropes supporting the rim which are spliced and yoked together to end in a single cord which allows the finished piece to swing freely (see Diagram D and Diagram E).

The top of the knotting is formed by a circle of steel rod. The working cords used were No. 170 cotton seine twine, hitched to the rod in usual fashion. Two rows of alternating square knots were tied with the heavy ropes passing between the knots. Turk's heads applied to the ropes keep the rim from slipping (Diagram F).

F.

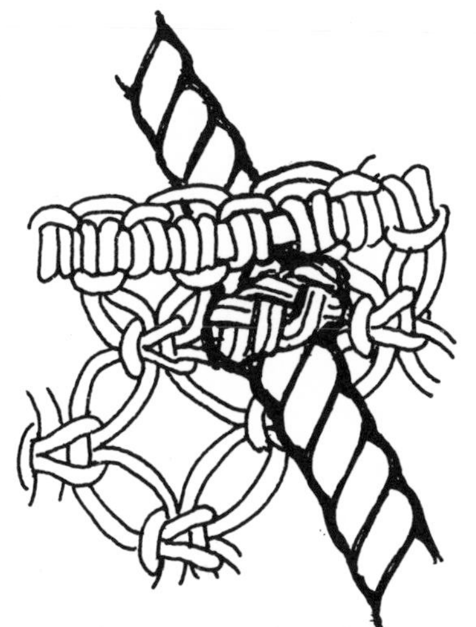

G.

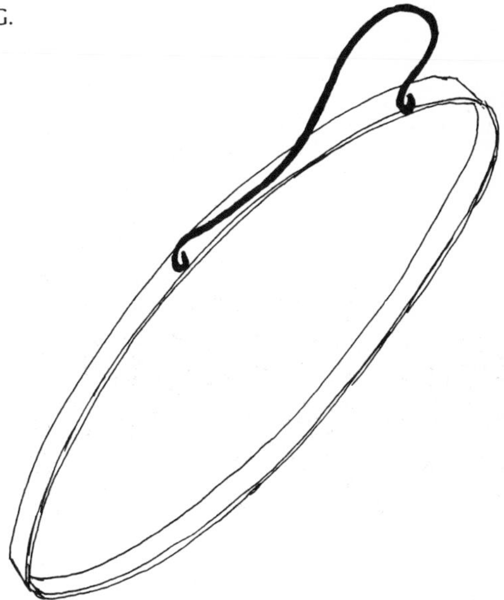

H.

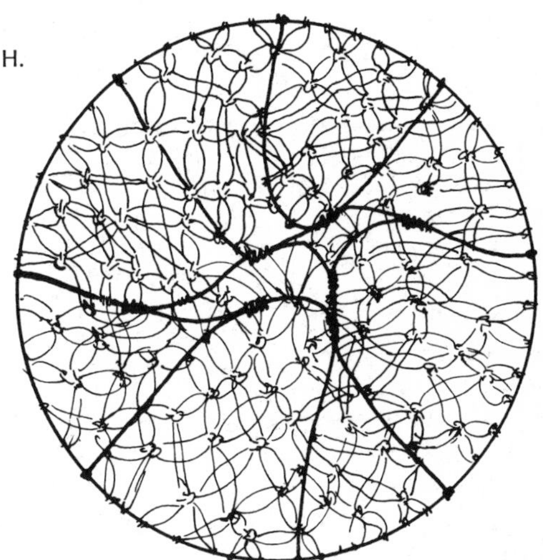

As the knotting was worked down, various openings and patterns were tied in to make a pleasing pattern when viewed from the inside of the swing. On one side of the rim we made a sort of access port, for sandwiches, by bringing the knotting out over a U-shaped metal form, secured to the rim by knotting (Diagram G).

Most of the working cords ended by clove hitching over the rim, with about one cord in four continuing over the rim to make the bottom of the swing. The knotting of the bottom was done in a free style with plenty of weaving of cords to make a surface with give for comfort (Diagram H).

Figure 24. Chair knotted onto a frame welded from ½″ steel rod.

Figure 25. Detail of knotting pattern in the chair back.

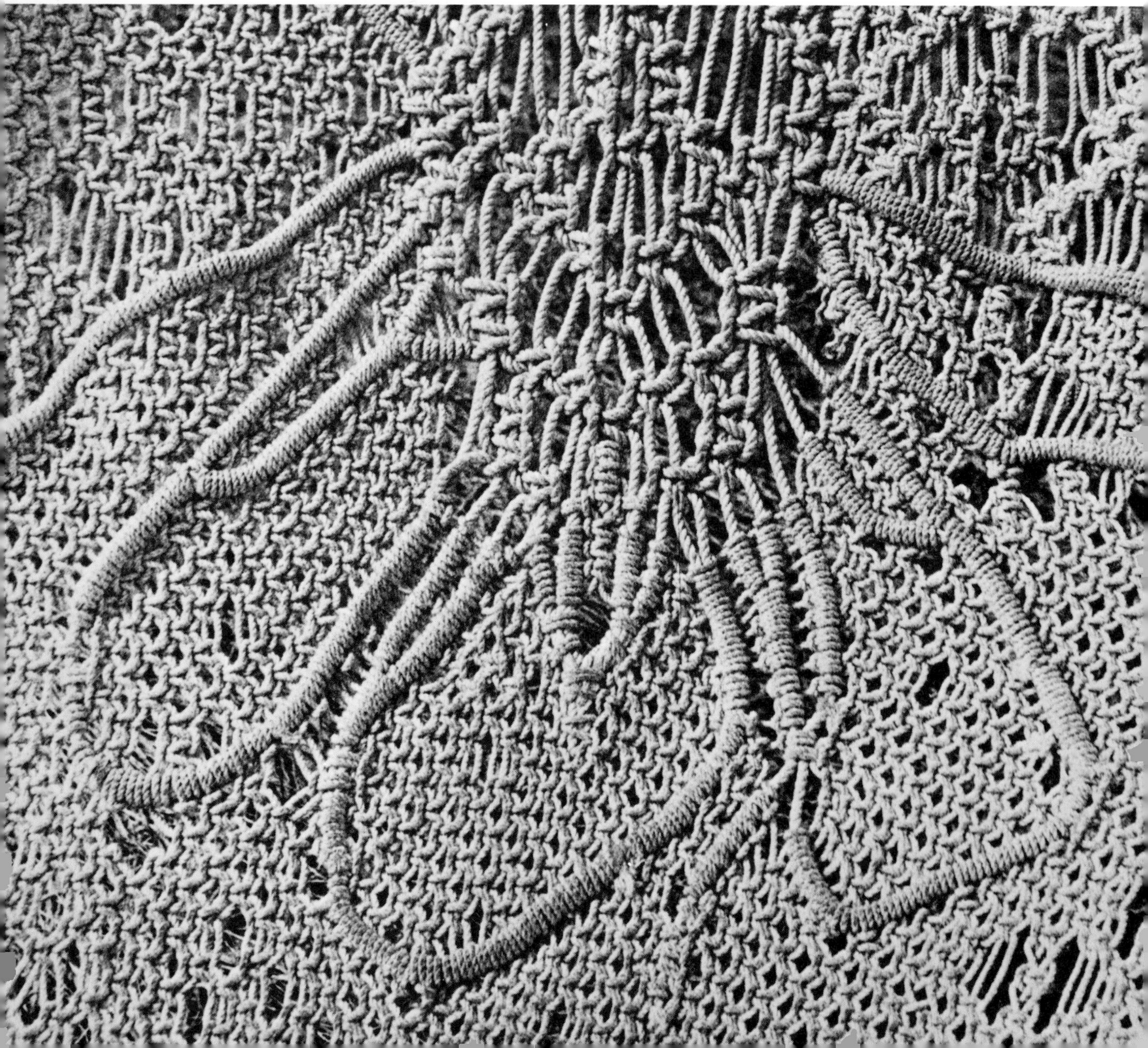

NOTES ON THE CHAIR

I.

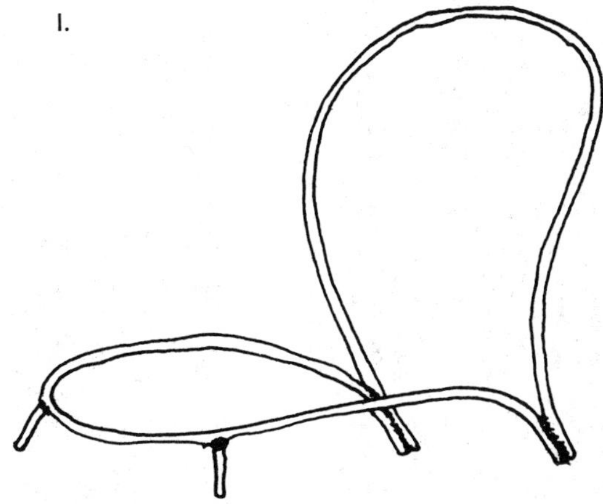

The frame is ½″ steel rod cold bent into shape and welded (Diagram I).

Once the frame is made, the knotting is done free-form, adapting it as needed to form the chair. If you use cotton cord, remember that it will stretch in use, so make the knotting tight, allowing for the sag which will develop with use.

Facing page: Figure 26. Wall hanging in cotton seine twine. (See also color photo, C-9.)

At right: Figure 27. The simple tassles used in this hanging are made as described earlier (pp. 66 and 67).

Below: Figure 28. Detail of the hanging. The heavy cords move through the hanging to make the pattern and are supported by the light cords.

Figures 29 and 30. Macrame play house for children and small adults. Approximately 5 feet across and 5½ feet high.

29

NOTES ON THE CASTLE

There are no specific instructions for a piece like this. About all you will need is two hundred pounds of cord, a strong ceiling, and time. Just about every technique mentioned earlier was used in this work.

30

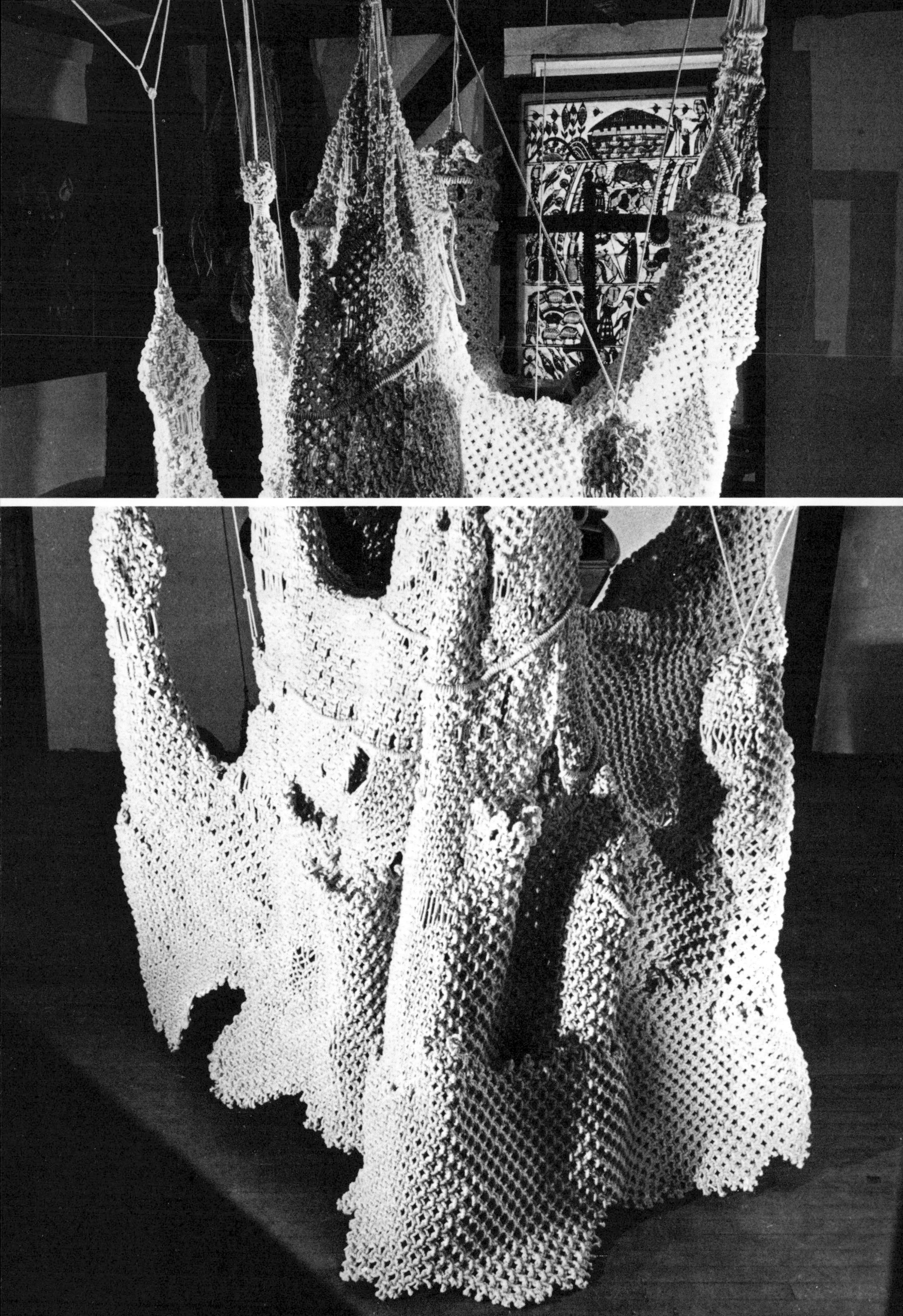

Figures 31 to 36. Details of the castle.

31

32

33

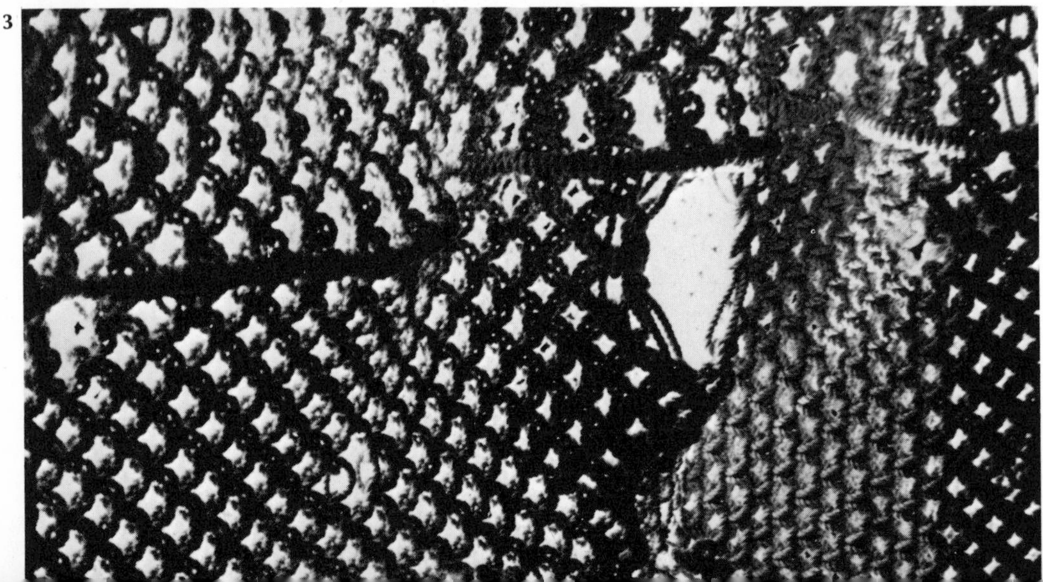

34

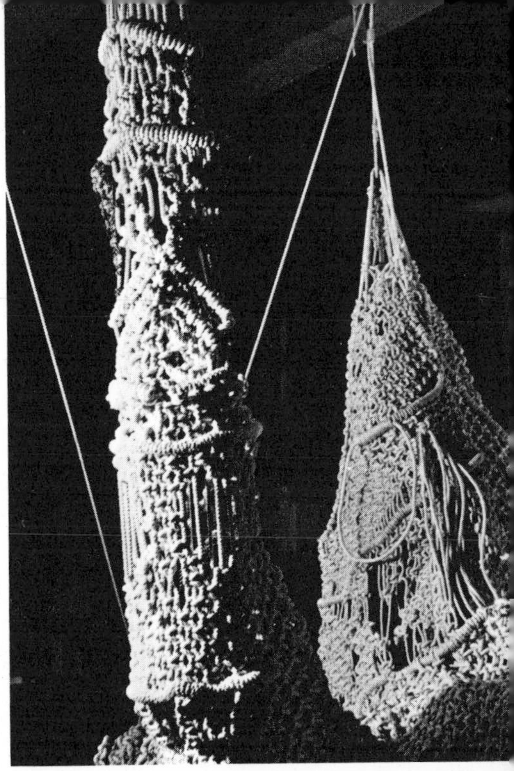

36

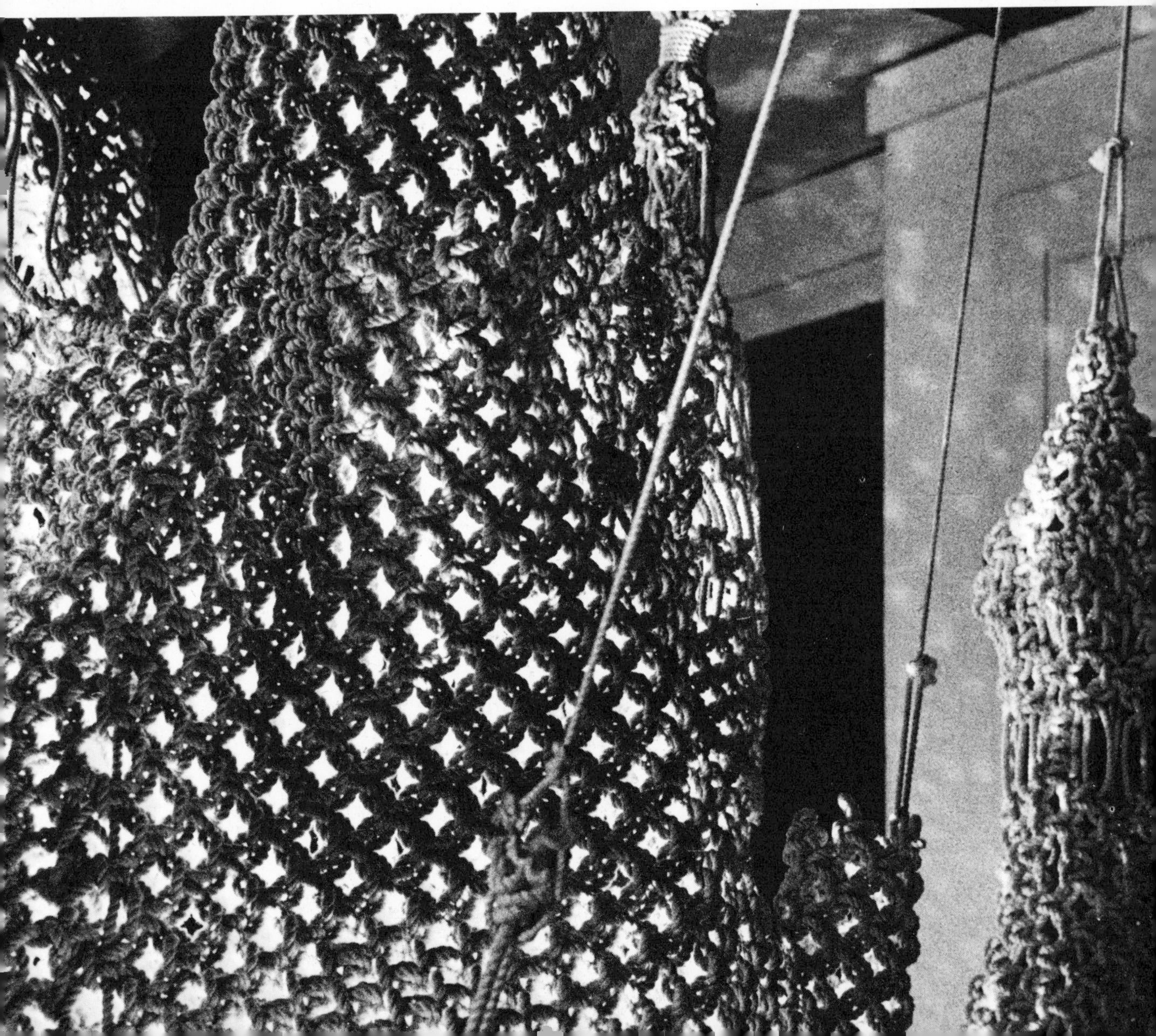

Figure 37. Detail photo of a hanging lamp in progress.

SECTION

3

This section presents some advanced rope work techniques and some other information we have found useful.

73. Installing a light-bulb socket on a lampshade holder.

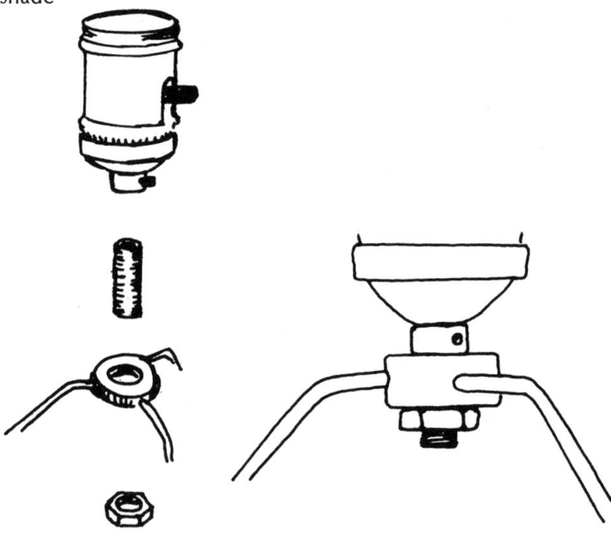

WIRING LAMPS

When you make a knotted lamp or lampshade, be sure that the cord you use is fireproof or fire resistant. Design the lamp so the cord will never touch or be too close to a light bulb, or cover the bulb with a chimney or glass globe to prevent accidental contact with the string.

Appliance repair shops and hardware stores will often have a stock of lamp chimneys and bases which can be used in lamps. The bulb sockets and bases must be securely bolted to the shade holder as shown in Diagram 73.

Knotted lamps or illuminated hangings may be controlled by a wall switch or by a switch on the hanging itself. In order to sensibly design and tie a lamp you must have some knowledge of wiring. Fixtures mounted on the wall or ceiling should be installed by a qualified electrician, but you must know how it's done so you can design the fixture properly.

In home electric wiring, two wires are the minimum required for a lamp to light or an appliance to operate. Modern house wiring uses a three-wire grounded system in which plugs have three prongs instead of two and outlets have three holes.

For convenience, in home wiring you may think of there being one wire through which current flows to an appliance and a second through which it returns to its source. House wiring is color coded to identify each wire. In the older system, there are two wires in each cable—one white wire (termed the ground) and one black wire (termed the hot wire). The white wire is connected to the earth at the point of entry into the house, providing a place for current to flow harmlessly in the event of a malfunction. The modern three-wire system has a second ground wire, color-coded green or left bare, which is also connected to earth at the service entrance. The second ground does not carry current during normal operation, unlike the white wire, and serves as an extra safety measure in the event of a malfunction. House wiring may be thought of most simply as depicted in Diagram 74.

A grounded wiring system provides essential protection against shock from appli-

74. Simplified diagram of house wiring showing the older two-wire system (above) and the modern three-wire system (below).

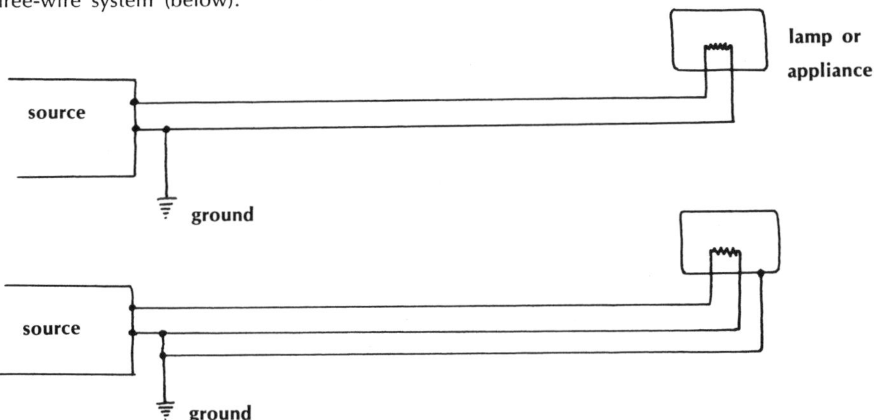

ances which are defective. If, for example, the black wire to a washing machine motor chafed through its insulation and contacted the metal cabinet of the machine, the entire machine would be "hot." If the white wire had also chafed and contacted the machine cabinet, the electricity would pass harmlessly to earth through the white wire. But if the white wire were not in contact with the cabinet, electricity would tend to flow through a person touching the cabinet as if seeking another route to earth. The addition of the third wire, the ground wire, makes it possible to attach it to the case of the machine, so that an alternate route to earth is provided for the electricity and a person touching a defective machine would not be shocked.

A lamp is a sort of appliance. The black and white wires carry current to and from the bulb. If a lamp has a metal case or a metal framework, those metal parts are often grounded through the third wire, especially in ceiling or wall-mounted fixtures (Diagram 75).

75. Diagram showing how a lamp with a metal frame is grounded in the three-wire system of house wiring.

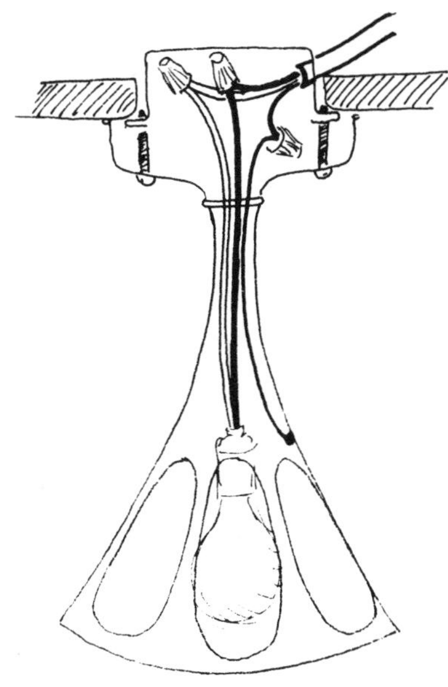

76. Various electric wires (top to bottom):
1. Single strand twisted copper wire, lamp cord —size 16 or 18.
2. Double strand twisted copper wire, lamp cord—size 16 or 18.
3. Double strand cable, solid copper, house wiring.
4. Double strand cable, solid copper with ground wire—house wiring.

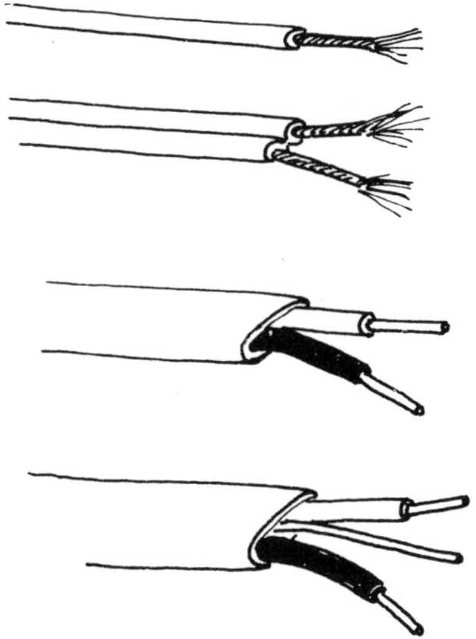

For standing lamps, particularly those made of wood or other nonconducting material, grounding is not necessary. The cords used for macrame do not conduct electricity, so it is not necessary to wire the usual macrame lamp with a three-wire system.

You should know something about wiring in order to buy supplies for your lamp.

The ability of a wire to carry electricity is related to its diameter; the larger the diameter, the more current it can carry. The thickness of the insulation around a wire determines the voltage the wire can safely handle. Since most home wiring is 110 to 120 volt, except for heating, ranges, hot-water heaters, and the like, you need not be concerned when shopping for wire, since most lamp cord will be adequate for home voltages. Wiring sold in stores should display an underwriters laboratories tag stating that it is approved for use at a certain voltage and amperage. (Amperage is a measure of current flow). Also, the wiring should carry a printed label stating the size of the wire. For lamps, No. 16 wiring is adequate, unless the lamp contains many bulbs, in which case the next larger size, No. 14, should be used. Most homes are wired with No. 14 and No. 12 wire in the household circuits for average usage, excluding heavy appliances. Lamp cord is usually No. 16 stranded copper wire covered with a plastic insulation and available in many colors and finishes. It may be purchased by the foot as a double or single wire (Diagram 76).

When your lamp is to be plugged into a wall receptacle, the wire should be of the double type with an underwriters laboratories approved plug on the end. You may install your own plug, but we often buy an extension cord, cut off the receptacle end, and use the cord to wire the lamp. By using an extension cord, you will have a plug permanently molded on the end of the cord (Diagram 77).

If the lamp is to be installed on a wall or ceiling, no plug is needed since the wires will be attached directly to the house wiring by the electrician. Later we will discuss how a hanging lamp is safely suspended from a ceiling.

Usually we wire a lamp after the tying is

77. Cut the socket end off an extension cord to make a lamp wire.

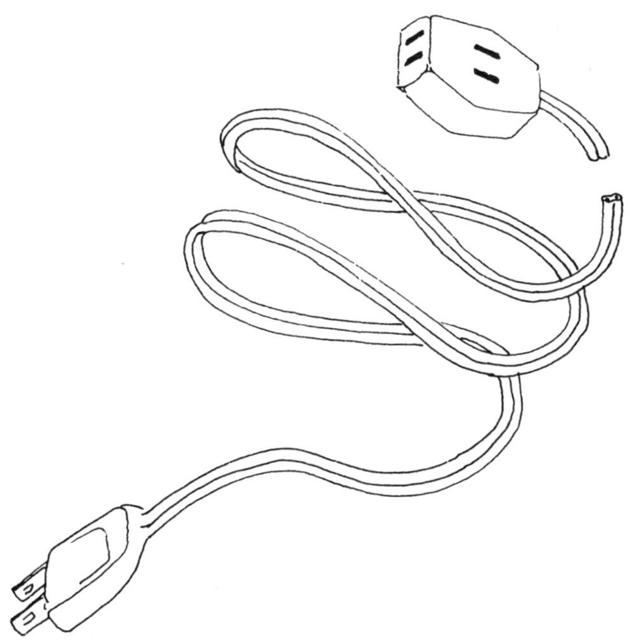

78. Lamp sockets: Candelabra base (left) and Edison base (right).

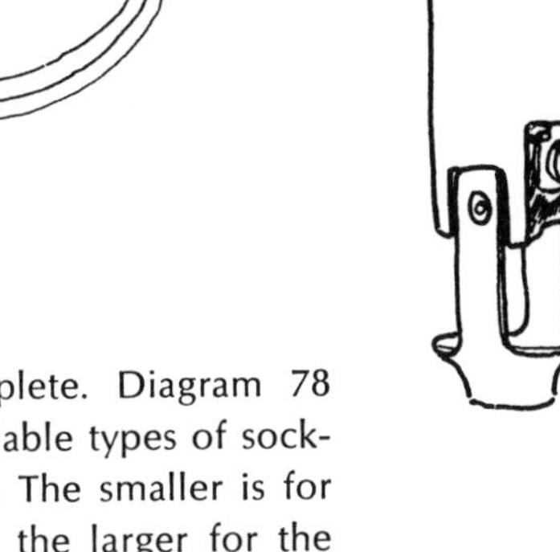

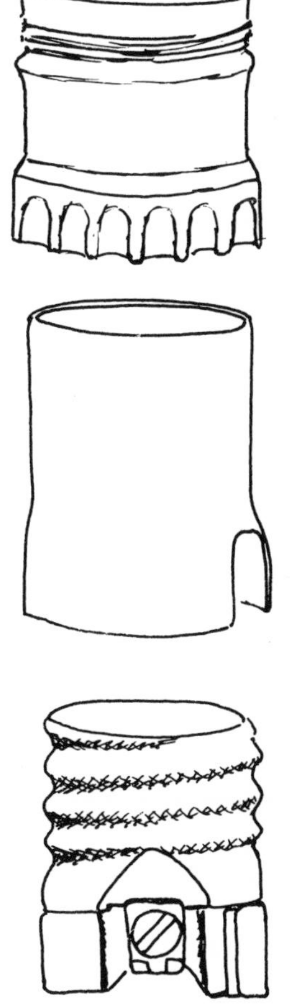

complete, or nearly complete. Diagram 78 shows two commonly available types of sockets for electric light bulbs. The smaller is for the candelabra base bulb, the larger for the Edison base bulb. Both types are wired similarly. A bulb socket will have on it a stamped message showing the underwriters approval and the voltage and wattage of the largest bulb to be used in that socket.

There will be two screw terminals for attaching the wires to the socket. One terminal will be silver colored and the other brass finished. The difference in color of the terminals is part of the color coding used in house wiring and, in this case, indicates that the white (grounded) wire is to be attached to the silver terminal and the black (hot) wire to the brass terminal.

When you wire the lamp, you will be using wire which is not color coded, so you should designate one strand as the black wire and mark it at each end with tape, especially if the fixture is to be wired directly into the house wiring, so the electrician can properly install it.

79. Wiring lamp sockets. Be sure to wrap the wire around the binding screw in the direction the screw turns to tighten.

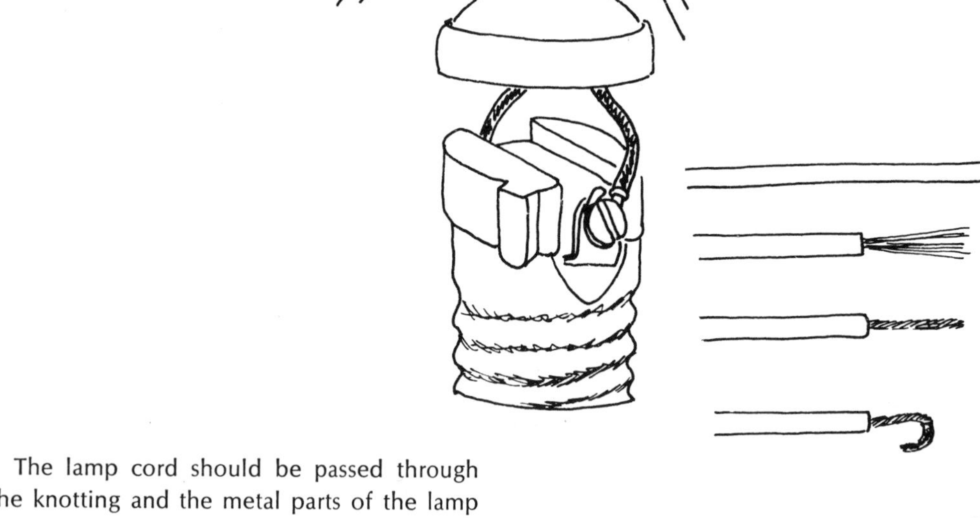

The lamp cord should be passed through the knotting and the metal parts of the lamp so it will not be exposed to excessive wear or chafing. Your hardware store will be able to provide you with the various fittings shown in Diagram 79.

When your lamp is to be hung suspended only from the wire, you will have to use special reinforced wire designed for that purpose. Wiring designed to carry the weight of a fixture will have a reinforcing fiber such as nylon in it. Special fittings which clamp the cord securely permit the attachment of a lamp directly to the cord. (Diagram 80).

When installing a lamp on the ceiling, you will need special hardware to carry the weight of the lamp. Most appliance stores sell kits containing the parts and instructions you will need to hang a lamp safely. A typical installation is shown in Diagram 81.

If you are at all unsure of your ability to wire safely a macrame lamp or illuminated hanging, do not hesitate to have it done for you by a professional. Any money you might save by doing it yourself is not worth the possible danger resulting from an improperly done job.

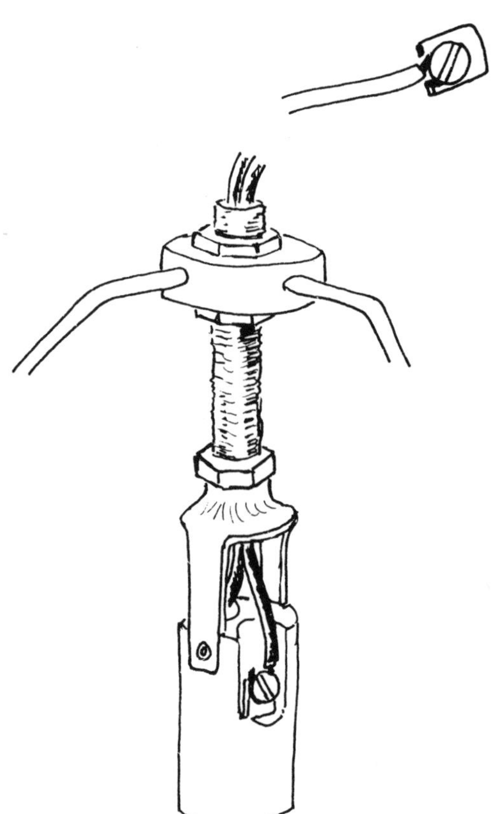

80. Use special clamping fittings to suspend a lamp directly from the wire. Be sure to use special reinforced wire which will support the weight of the lamp.

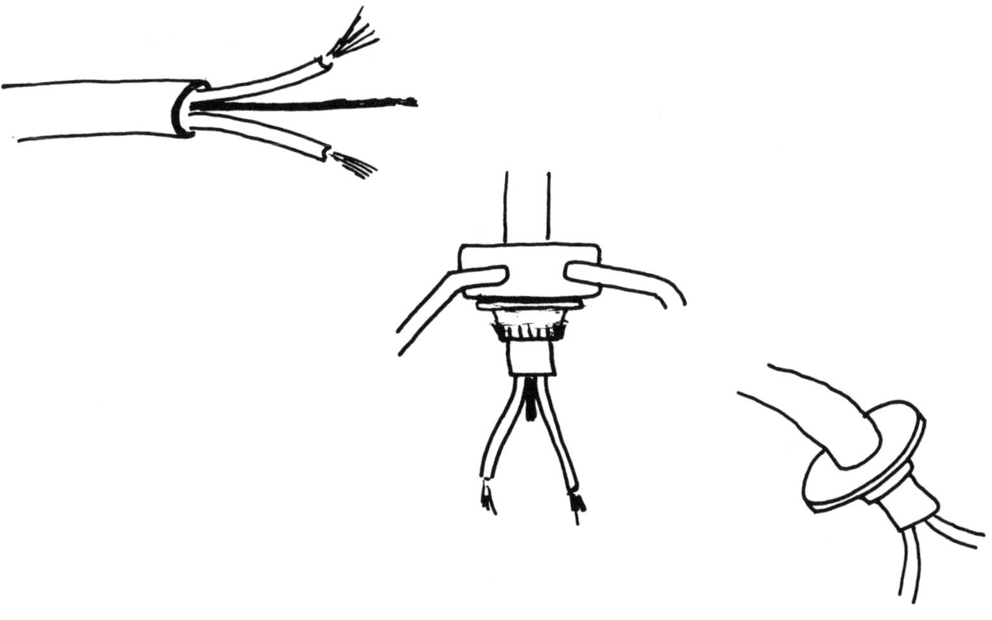

81. A typical lamp installation showing the appliance hanger bolted directly to the junction box.

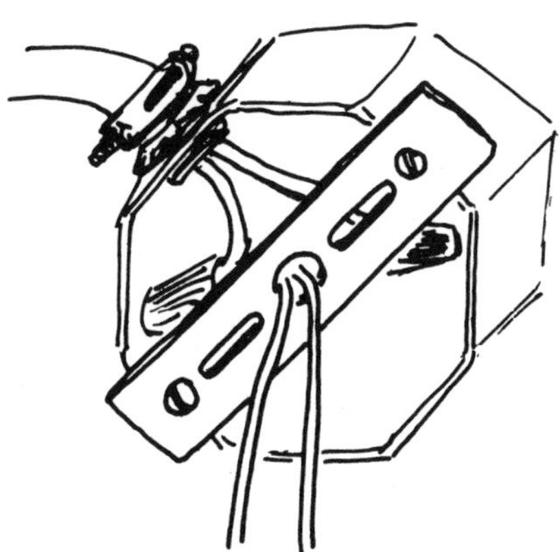

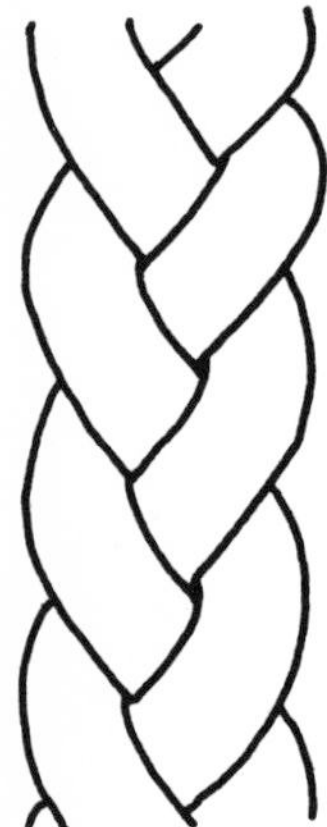

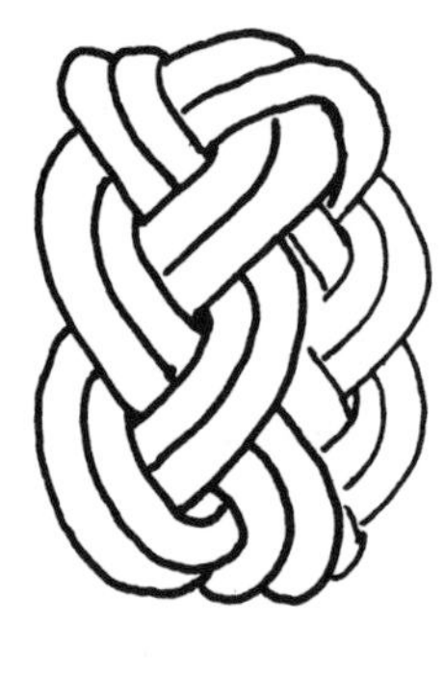

TURK'S HEAD KNOTS

82. The pigtail braid (left) and the turk's head related to it, shown one-, two- and three-ply.

Turk's heads are cylindrical knots which may be thought of as a variation of braiding. In the simplest three-part pigtail braid, each cord passes over and under the others in a weave which makes the braid stable. The same weaving occurs in turk's heads and makes them stable. (Diagram 82.)

Traditionally, turk's heads are usually doubled or tripled by passing the cord through the pattern a second or third time, paralleling the first and second strands.

There are hundreds of turk's head knots of varying complexity and size. Each knot may be named according to a system, and to name a turk's head is to know how to tie it, in most cases, since many of the complex knots may be tied by expanding the simpler ones.

A turk's head is specified by giving the number of times the cord passes around the cylinder, and the number of times it passes back and forth across the cylinder. We use the term "part" to refer to each passage around the cylinder and "turn" to indicate the number of times the cord appears at the rim of the knot to reverse direction and return to the knotting. The simplest turk's head is named 3 part, 4 turn (No. 3 in Figure 38). More complicated knots are tied in two ways: Increasing the number of turns and/or increasing the number of parts. A turk's head may have any number of parts, greater than 3, but will always have an even number of turns, greater than 4. Figure 38 shows 3 part turk's heads of 4 turns, 8 turns, 14 turns, and turk's heads of 4 parts, 5 parts, 6 parts, and 8 parts.

Figure 38. Turk's head sampler. From left to right:
1. 3 part 14 turn knot.
2. 3 part 8 turn knot.
3. 3 part 4 turn knot.
4. 4 part 6 turn knot.
5. 6 part 10 turn knot.
6. 8 part 12 turn knot.
7. 5 part 8 turn knot.

All you must know in order to tie the turk's heads shown is how to tie the 3 part knot with its expansions to 5 parts, 7 parts, 9 parts, and so on, and how to tie the 4 part with its expansions to 6 parts, 8 parts, and so on.

The smaller knots may be tied over the hand, but more complex knots will require a tying jig. Diagram 83 shows a simple turk's head tying jig made from an old cardboard mailing tube about 4″ in diameter, or from an oatmeal box.

We will present in detail the 3 and 4 part turk's heads together with the basic expansions of each. When tying any turk's head, the working cord must end on the same side of the knot as the standing part for the knot to be complete.

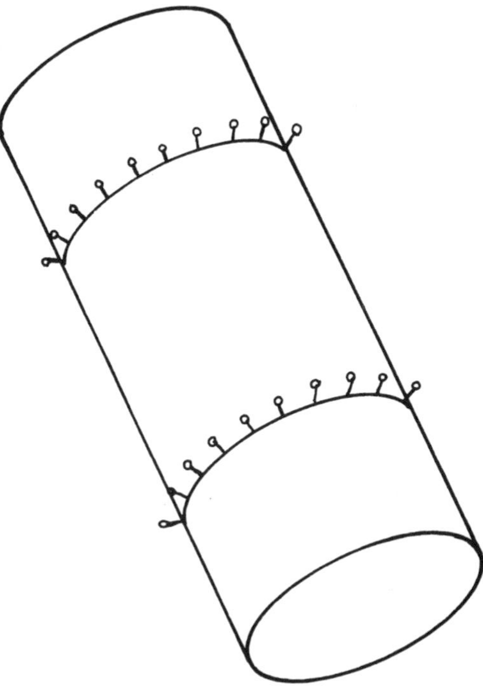

83. Tying jig for turk's heads made from an oatmeal container or a cardboard mailing tube.

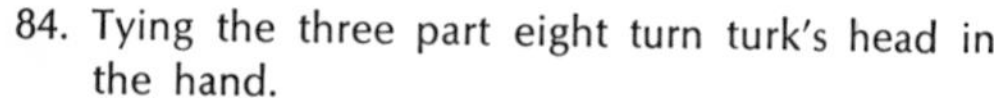

84. Tying the three part eight turn turk's head in the hand.

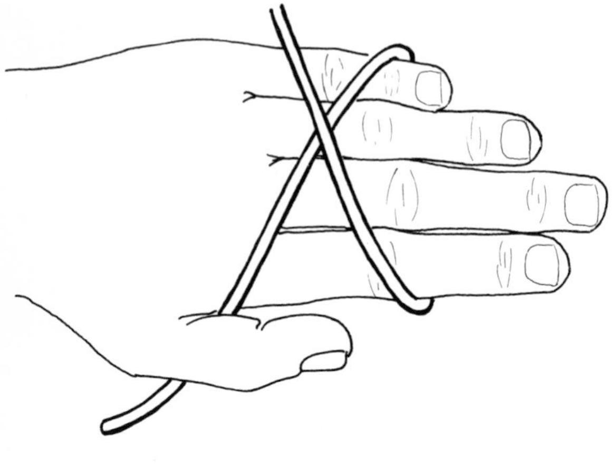

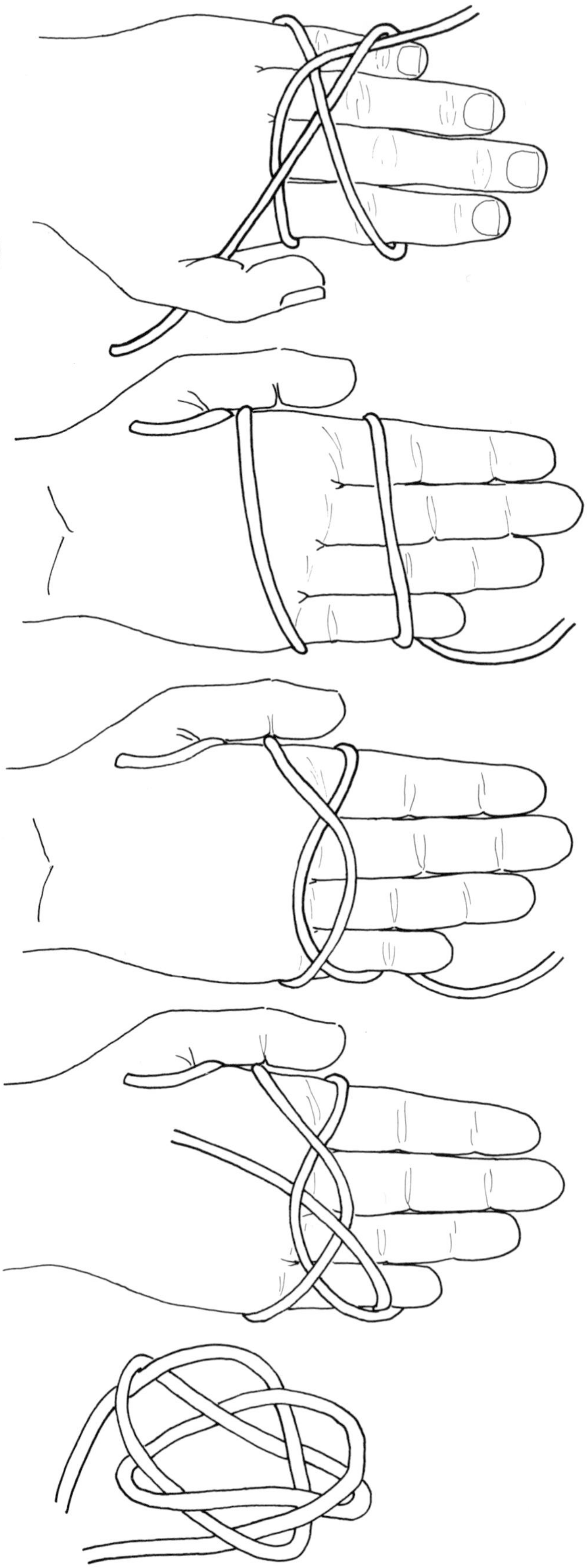

Three Part Turk's Heads

These knots are easiest to tie "in the hand" and may be tied in two ways. The first method is depicted in Diagram 84 and produces a 3 part 8 turn turk's head. This is the technique we use most often when tying turk's heads for use as decorative trim or tassels on rope because a turk's head of less than 8 turns is rarely useful for this purpose. The number of turns can easily be increased as shown in Diagram 85. The steps involved in increasing the turns are weaving to the right, crossing the loops, and weaving to the left. These steps increase the knot by 6 turns and may be repeated to make 3 part 14 turn, 20 turn, 26 turn knots, and so on.

85. Increasing the turns in a turk's head. Work the knot around to the back of the hand to make the pattern shown in the first drawing (A). Then weave the working cord to the right (B), cross the loops in the palm (C), and weave to the left (D).

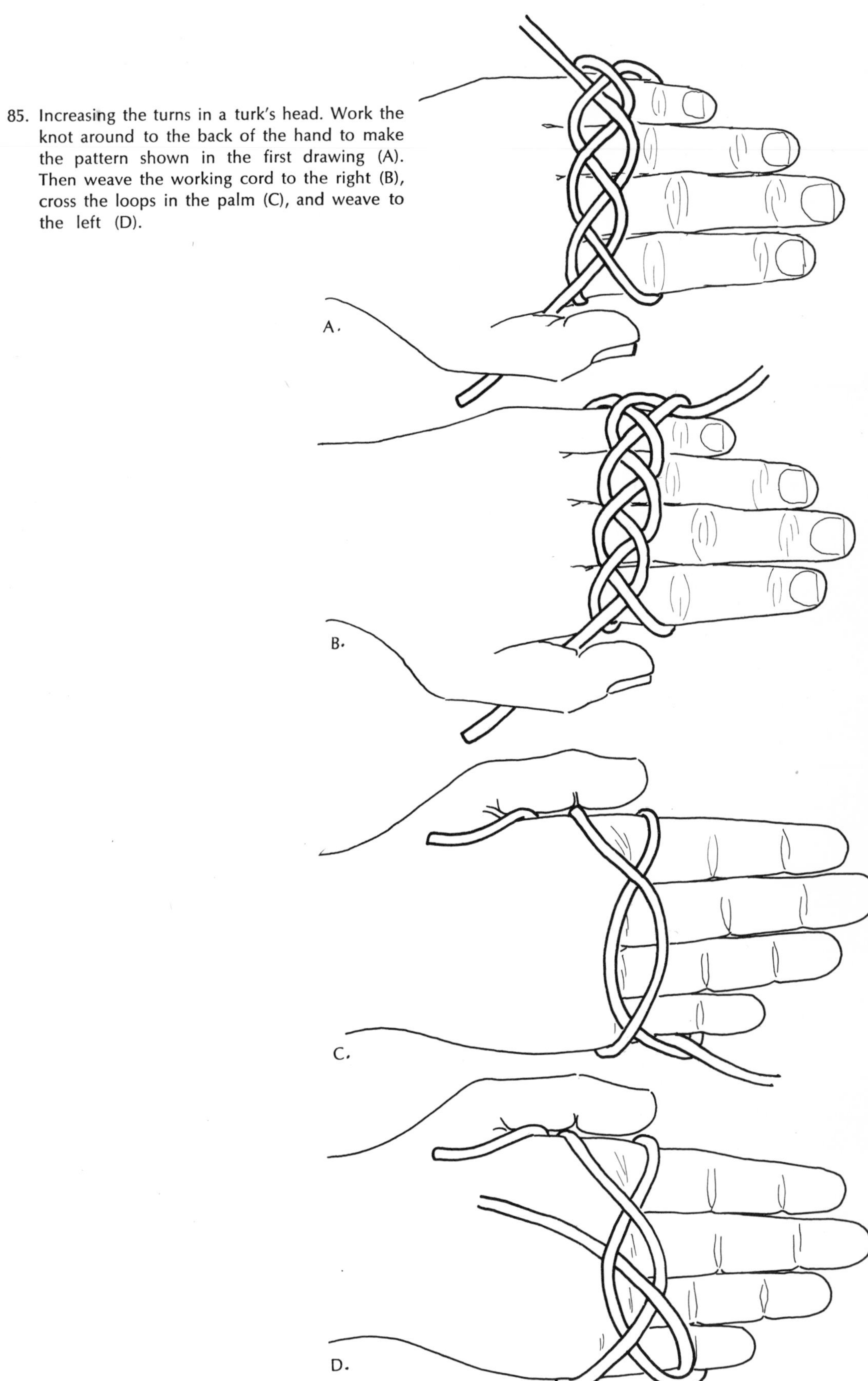

PHOTO SERIES D

Expanding the 3 part 4 turn turk's head:
1, 2, and 3. Tying the basic knot.
4, 5, and 6. Rolling the lower crossing around the palm to rearrange the knot to a form easier to expand.
7. Making the first weave for expanding the knot. This step is done for both expansions.

1

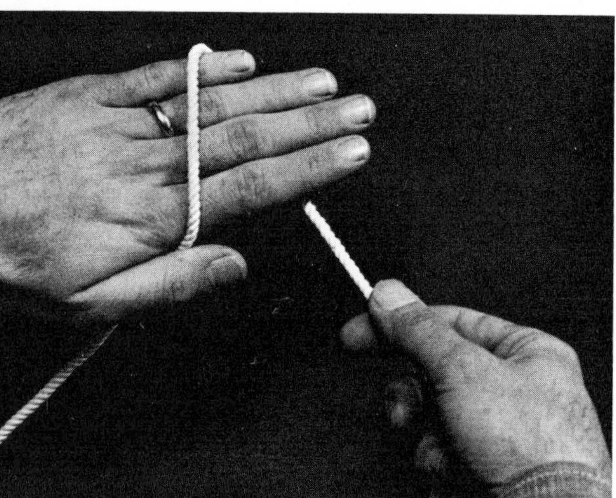

2

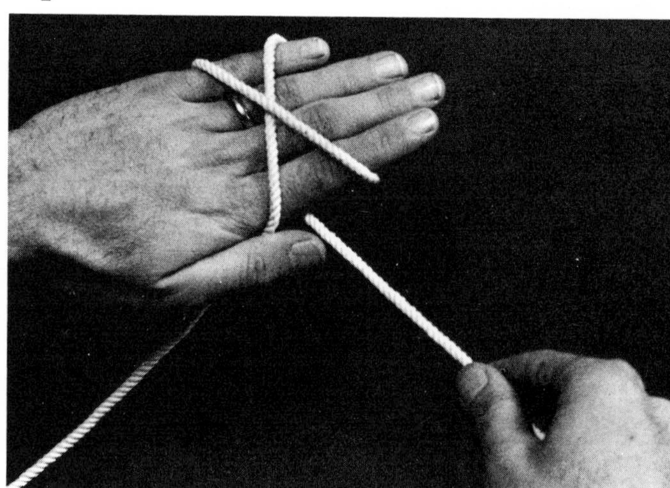

3

4

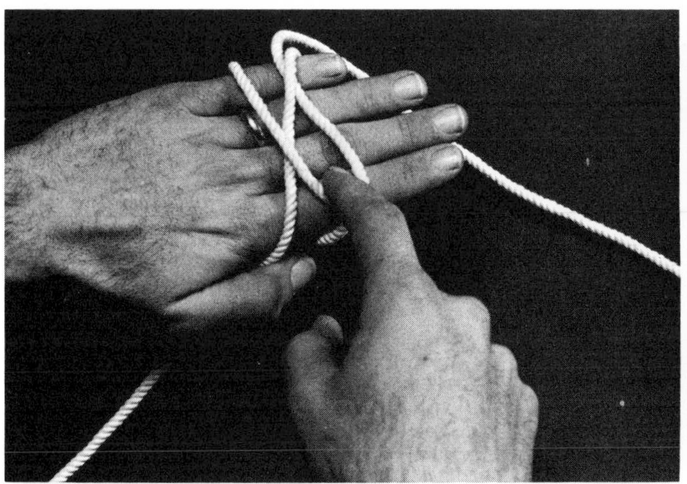

5

6

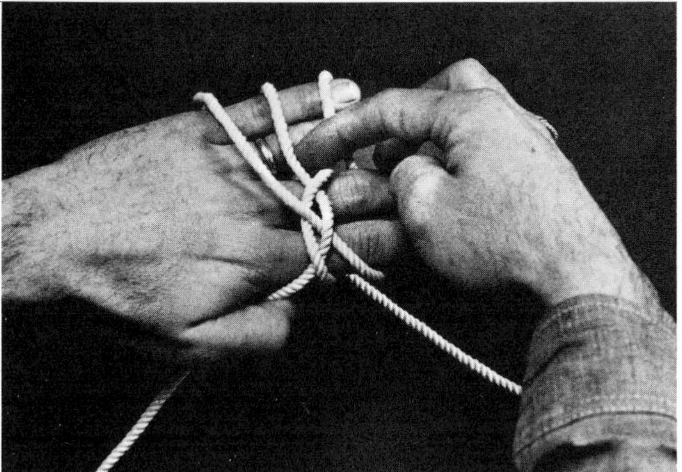

7

8, 9, 10, and 11. Tying the 3 part 10 turn knot by increasing the number of turns.

12–18. Expanding to the 5 part 8 turn knot from the knot shown in No. 7. Notice that the working end passes around the hand before each weaving, simultaneously increasing the number of parts and turns.

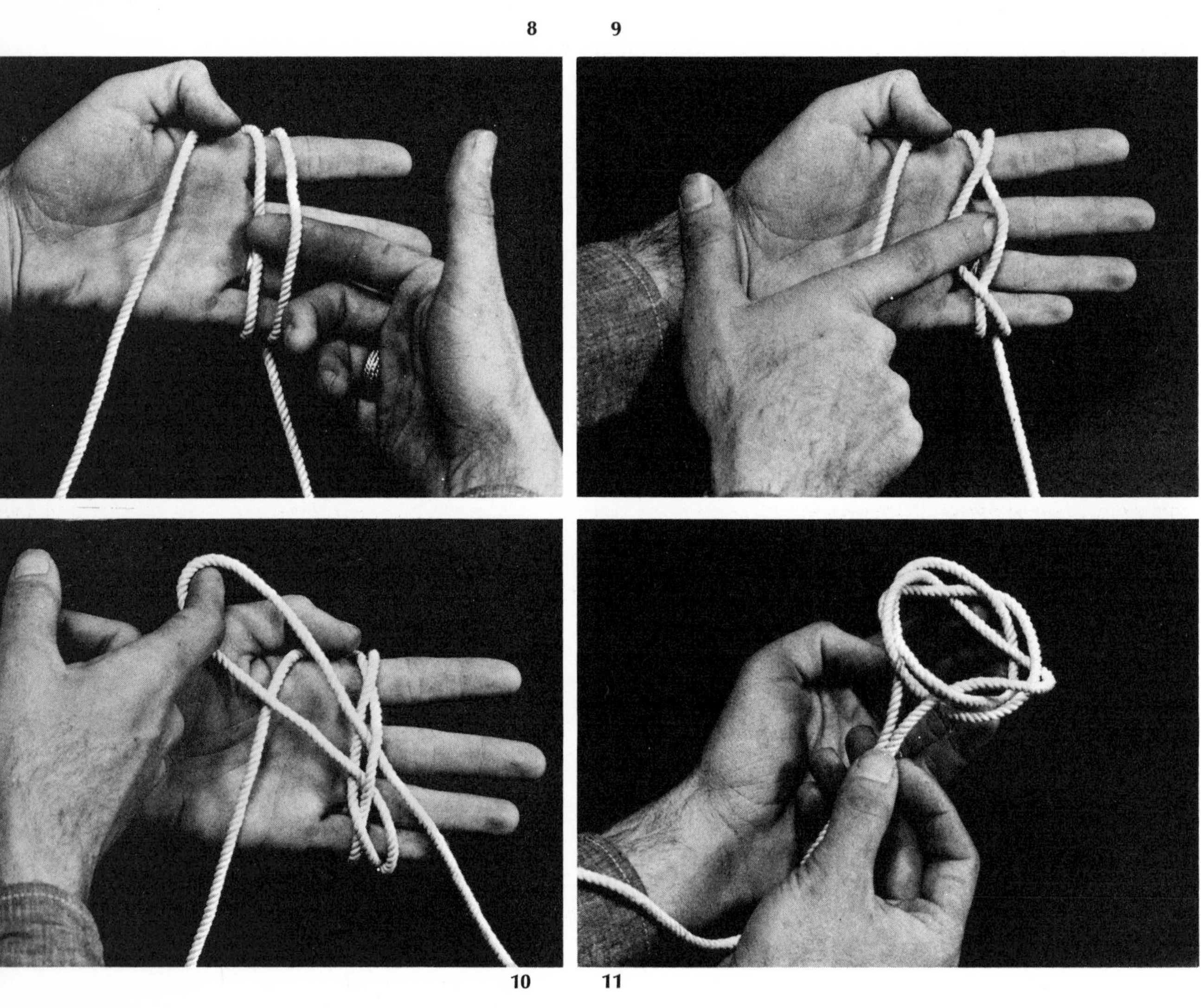

8 9

10 11

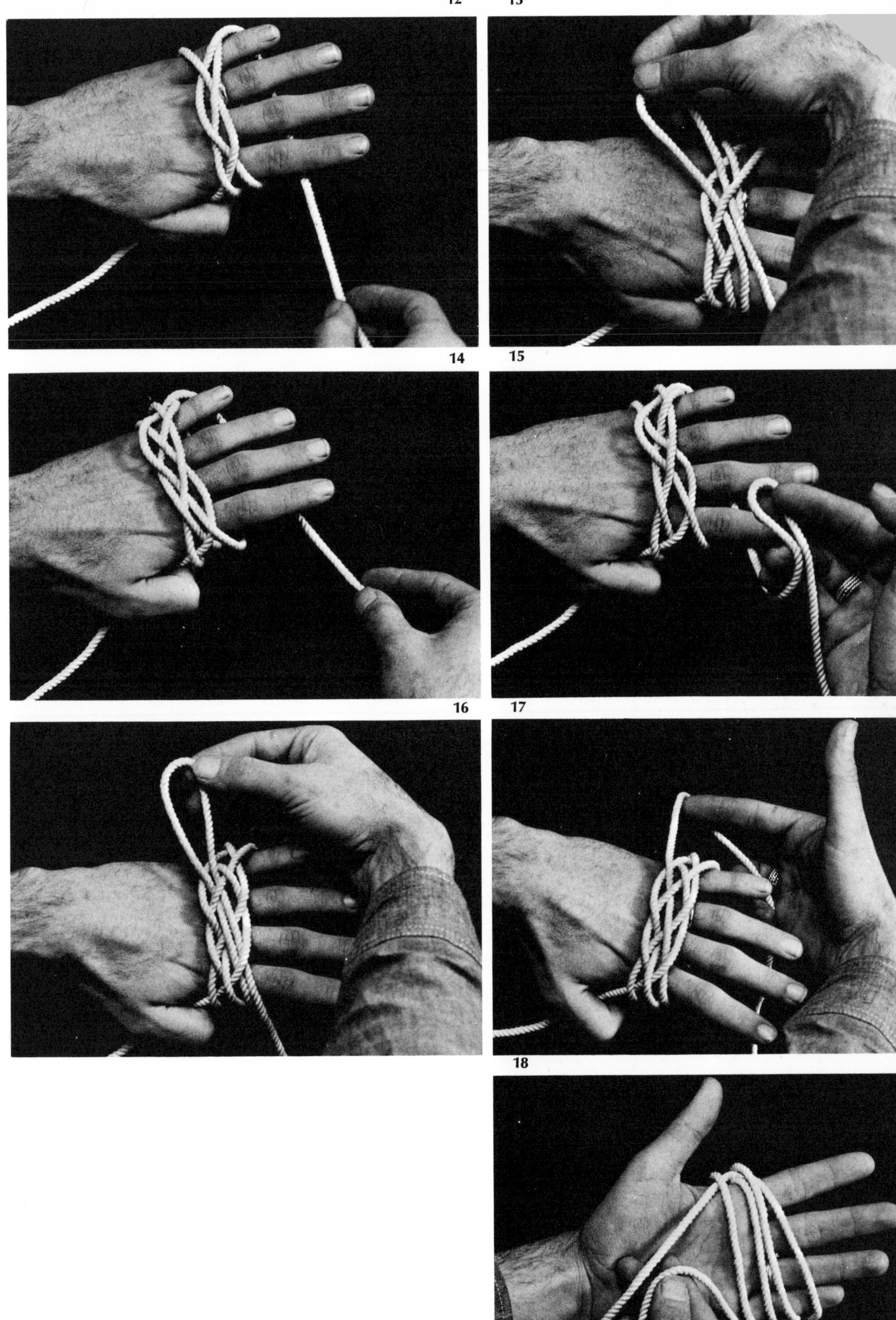
12
13
14
15
16
17
18

86. The three part, four turn turk's head is the simplest turk's head.

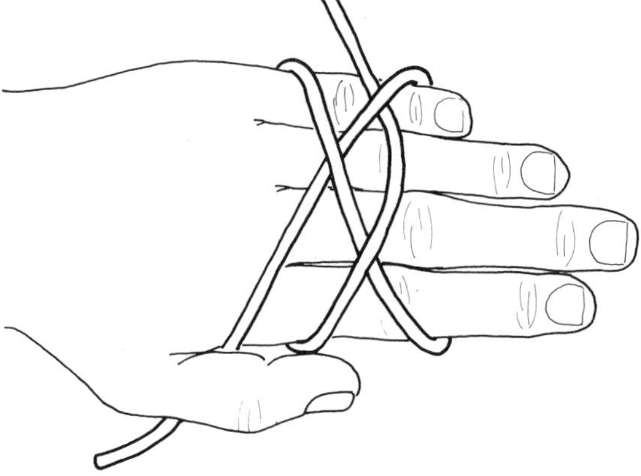

87. Expanding to a three part ten turn knot.

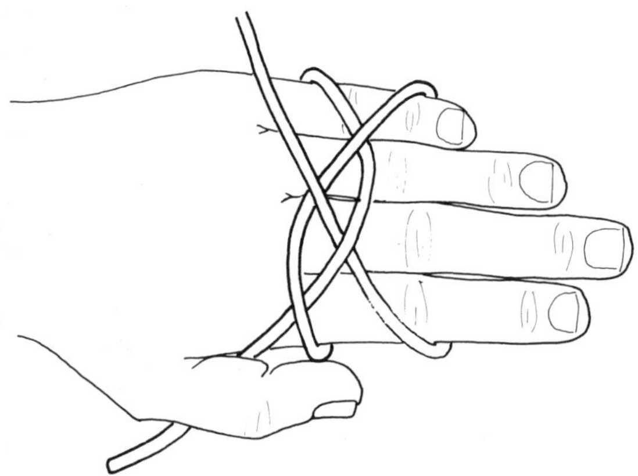

The second method of tying the 3 part turk's head is shown in Diagram 86. The basic knot in this case is the 3 part 4 turn knot, and it is also extended by increasing the number of turns as shown in Diagrams 87 and 88.

The method of expansion is similar—weaving, crossing of loops, and weaving—and results in an increase of 6 turns each time. This second method of tying 3 part turk's heads produces a series of knots with 4 turns, 10 turns, 16 turns, 22 turns, and so on, and is the method we use when tying turk's heads to be increased to a greater number of parts.

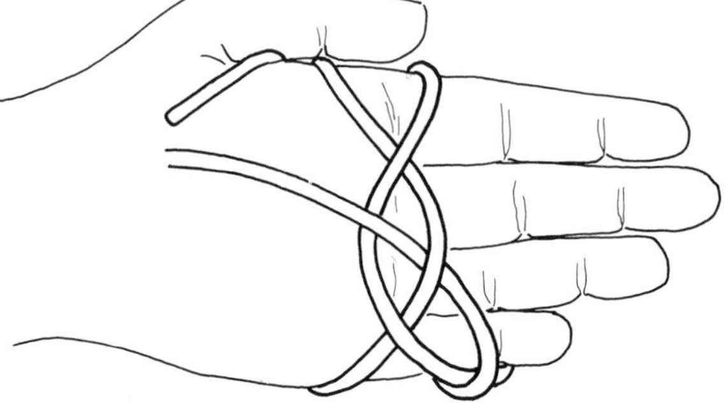

88. A second expansion produces a three part sixteen turn knot.

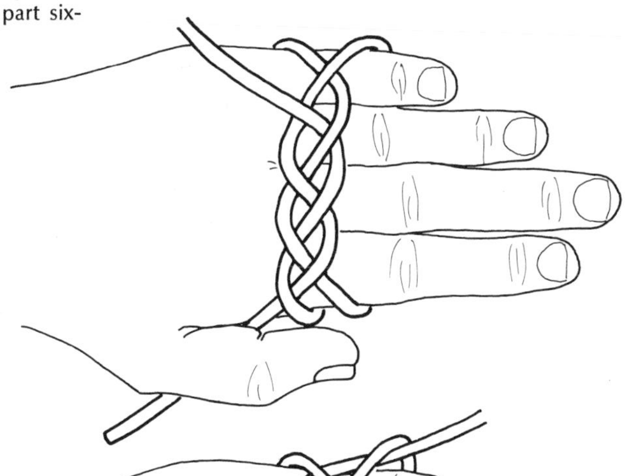

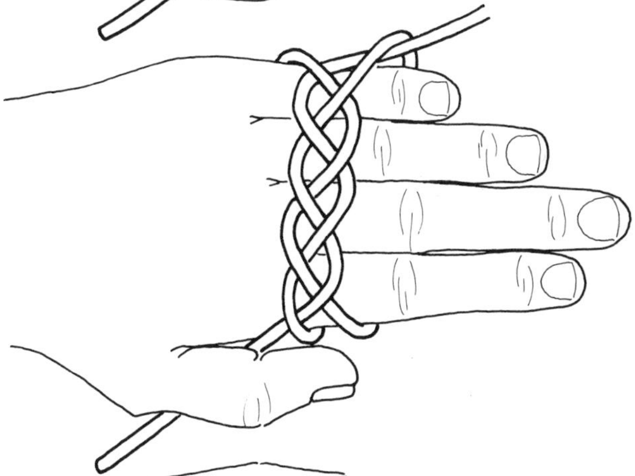

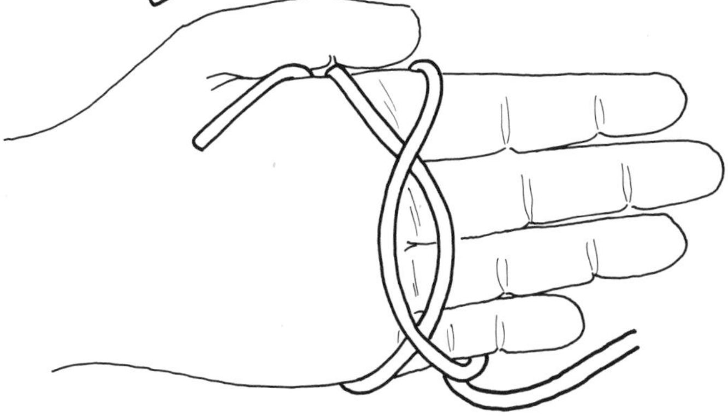

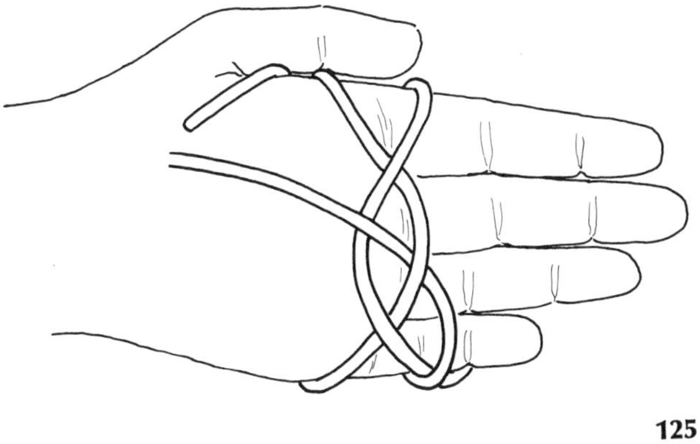

89. Increasing the number of parts in the three part knot to produce a five part knot with eight turns.

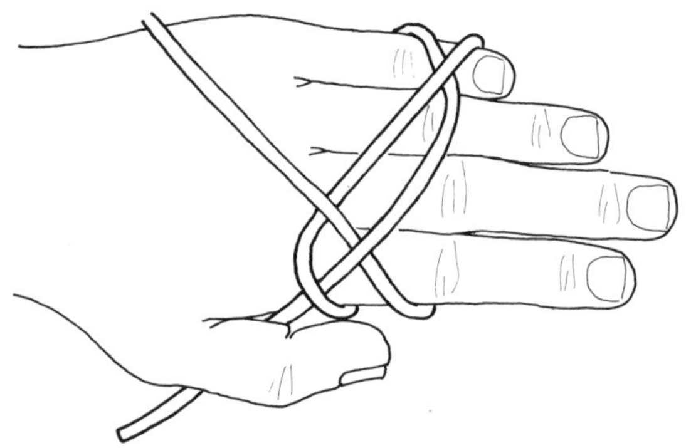

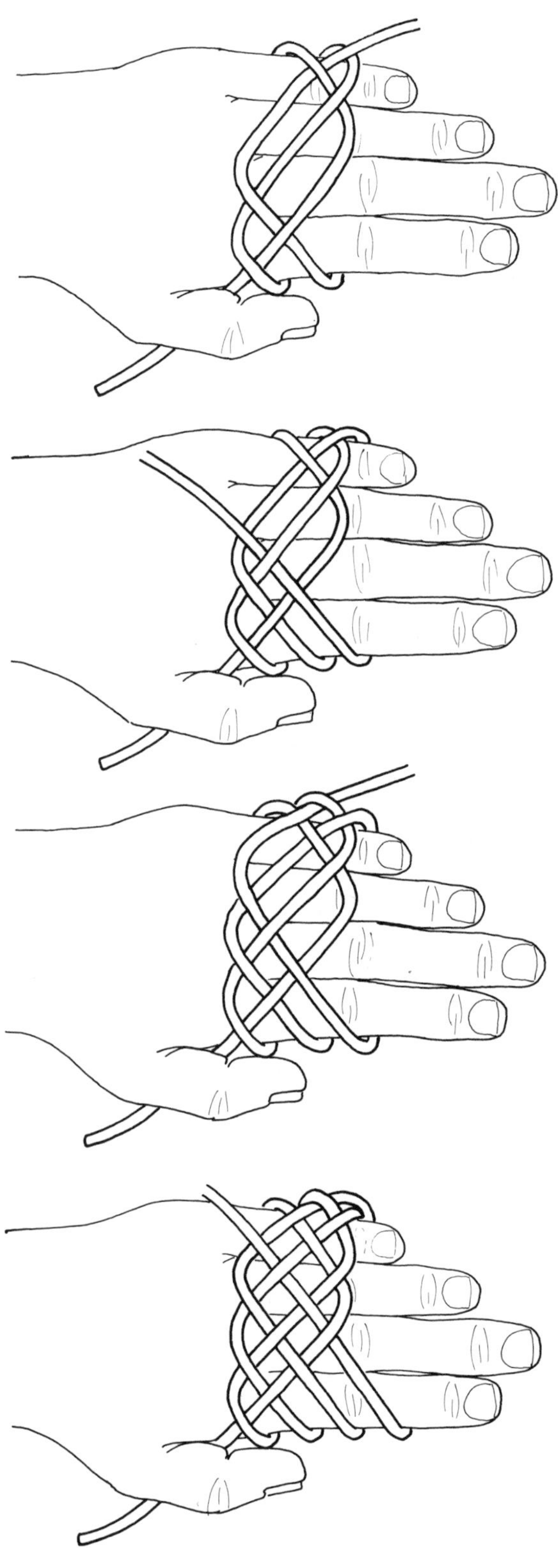

Although the first type of 3 part turk's head can also be increased, we prefer to expand the second type because it has fewer turns and is easier to expand. Diagram 89 shows the expansion of the 3 part 4 turn turk's head into the 5 part 8 turn turk's head. Whenever a turk's head is expanded, the number of parts is increased by two with each expansion, so the three part turk's head is the basis of a series of Turk's heads with odd numbers of parts—3, 5, 7, 9, and so on. A three part turk's head cannot be expanded into a turk's head with an even number of parts.

Turk's heads with an even number of parts begin with the 4 part 6 turn knot shown in Diagram 90. This knot expands into the 6 part 10 turn knot (Diagram 91), the 8 part 12 turn knot (Diagram 92), and so on.

A turk's head may be finished by gluing or side splicing each end to an adjacent strand.

90. The four part six turn turk's head.

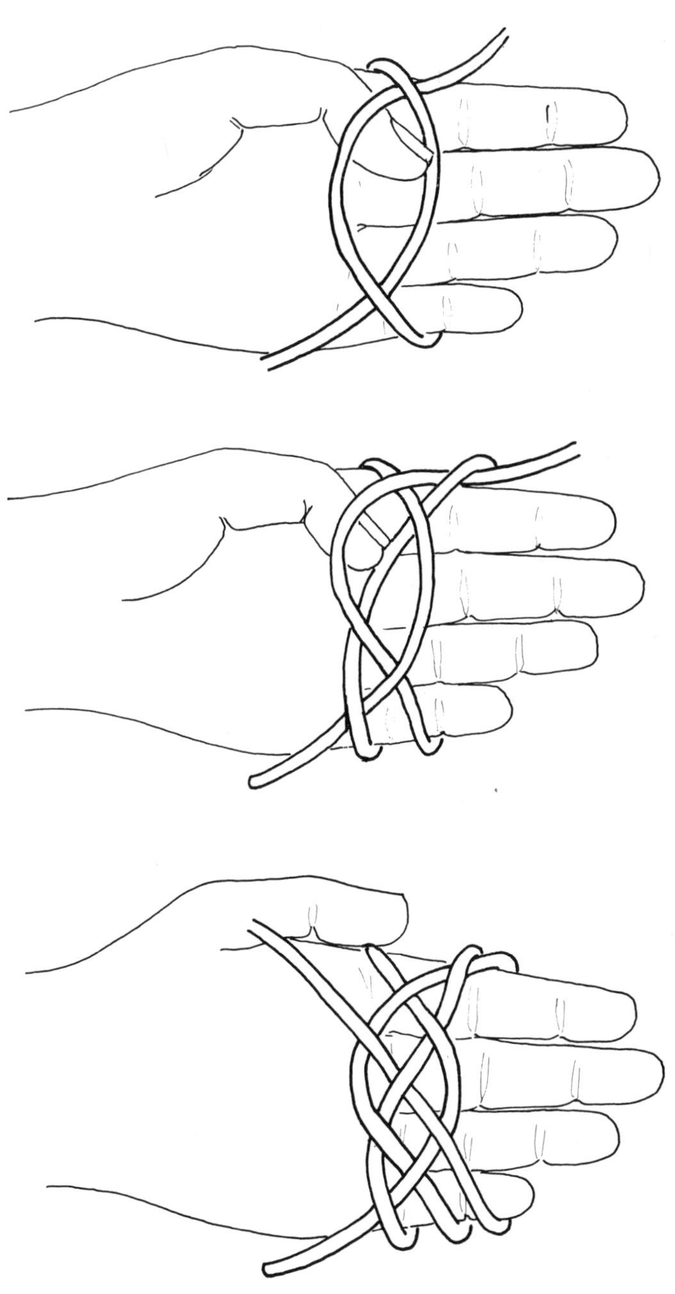

91. Expansion of the four part knot to the six part knot.

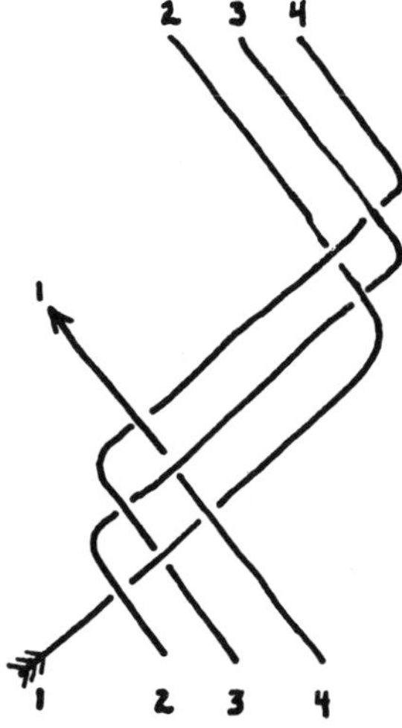

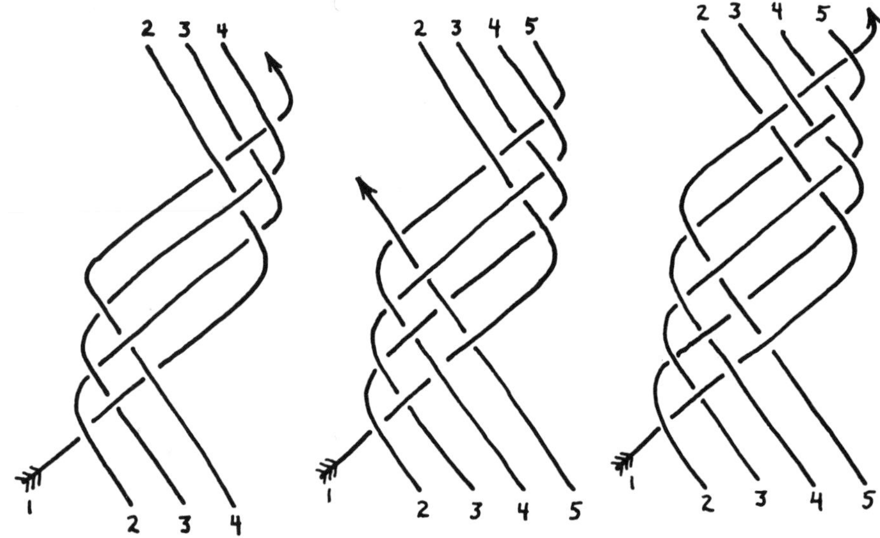

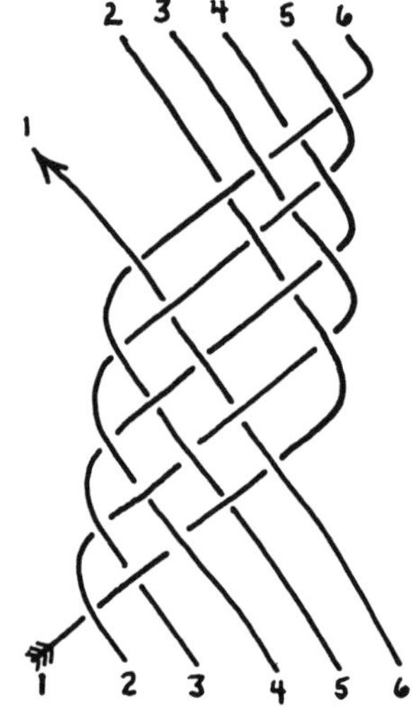

92. Expansion of the six part knot to the eight part knot.

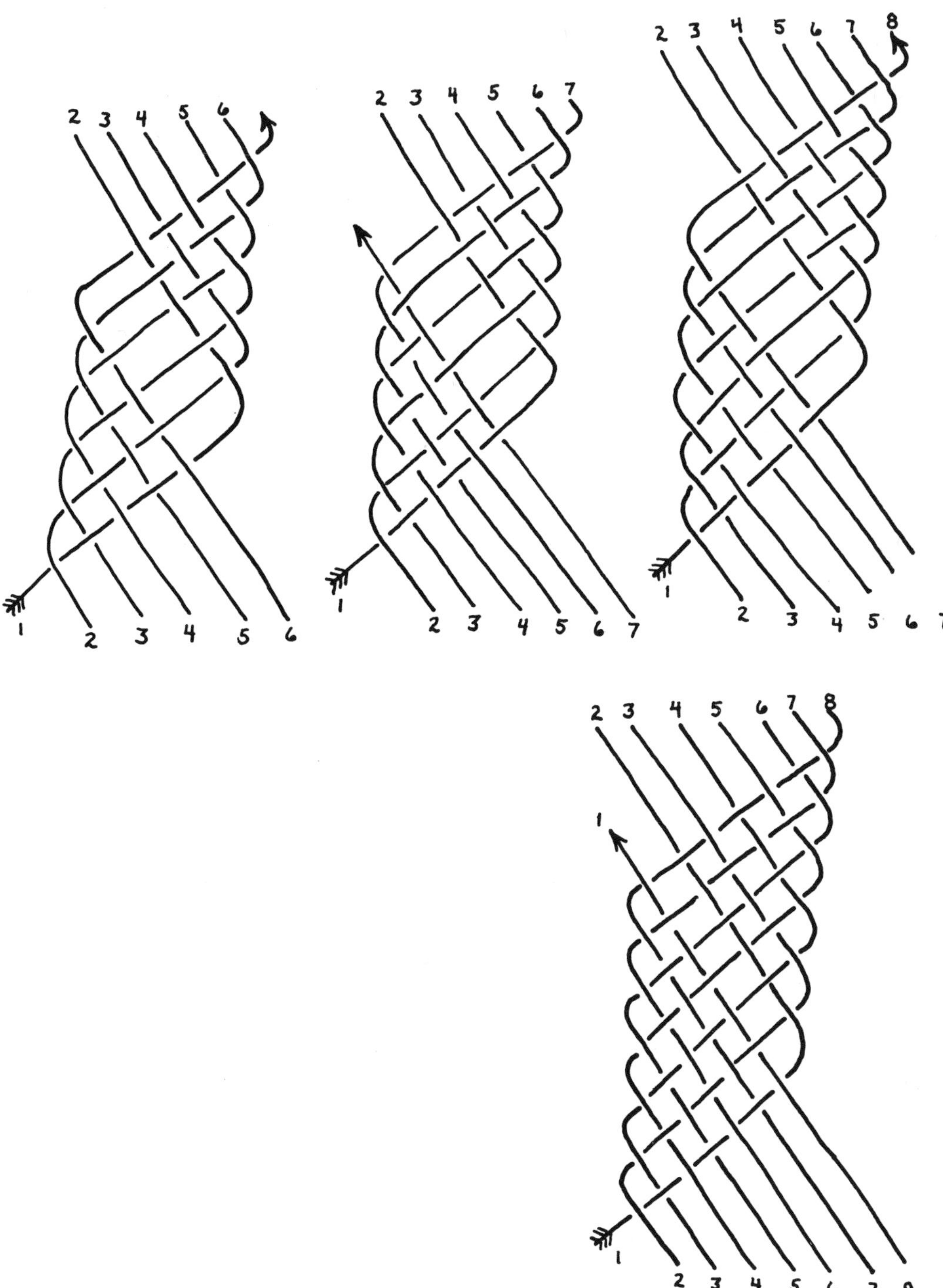

SPLICING

When two ropes or cords are to be joined, the strongest way to join them is by splicing.

The greatest strength of any cord lies in the direction of its component fibers (lengthwise) and in a knot, the pull on the rope is converted to force across the cord, which tends to break the fibers. A knot in string or rope decreases the strength of that cord by about 50 percent (see Diagram 93). You can prove this easily by using thread or light string. Take two lengths, say 18″ long, tie a simple overhand knot in one, and tug on each piece until it breaks. The knotted thread should break with much less pull. This is a trick known to many old-timers who knot a string so it will break where they want it to.

In a splice, however, the cords do not reverse direction, as in a knot, and a proper splice may leave as much as 75 to 85 percent of the strength of the cord intact.

In theory, splicing would be a good way to replace short cords in a macrame piece, but we have found that the extra time required to splice on a new cord is usually not justified. If, however, the piece cannot have the trimmed ends of the replaced cord hidden, splicing is a good means to replace cord with minimal evidence.

There are two basic types of splices used on twisted cord: the short splice and the long splice. The many other splices mentioned in nautical work are generally variations of these.

93. When two cords are joined by a knot, pull on the cord is directed across the fibers of the cord within the knot and thus a knotted rope is weaker than the intact rope.

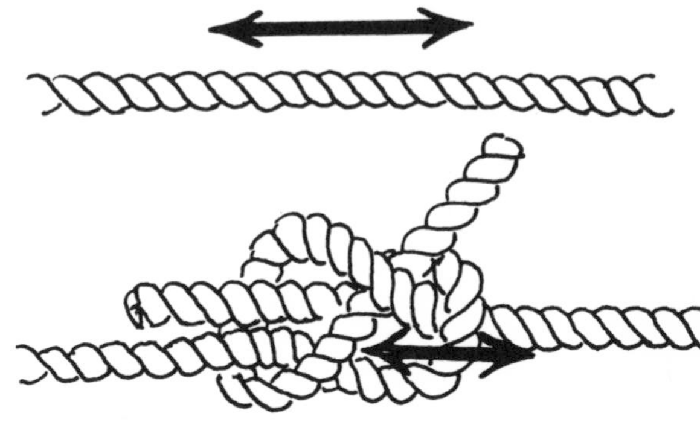

Figure 39. Back splice, eye splice, and short splice.

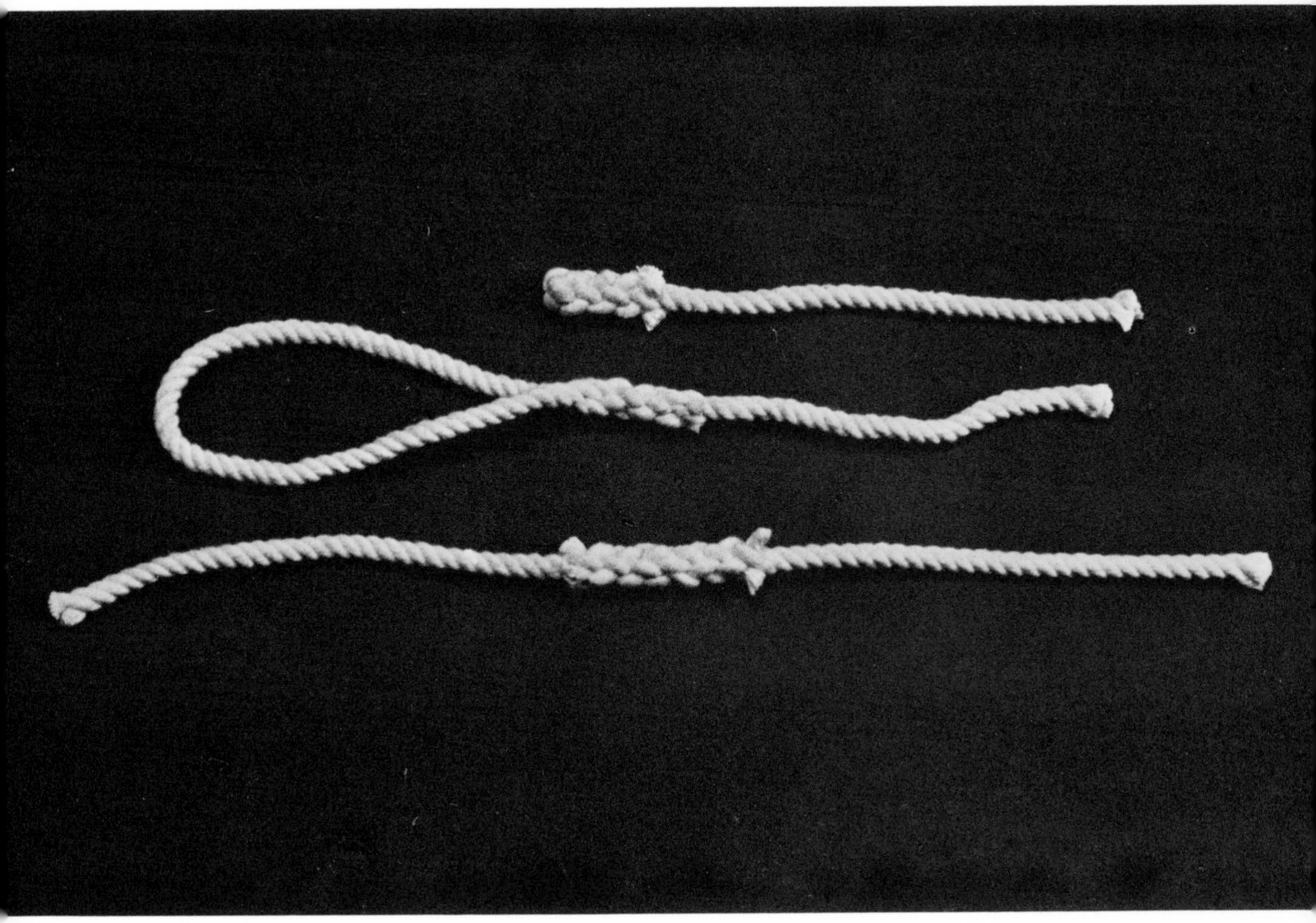

94. The short splice.

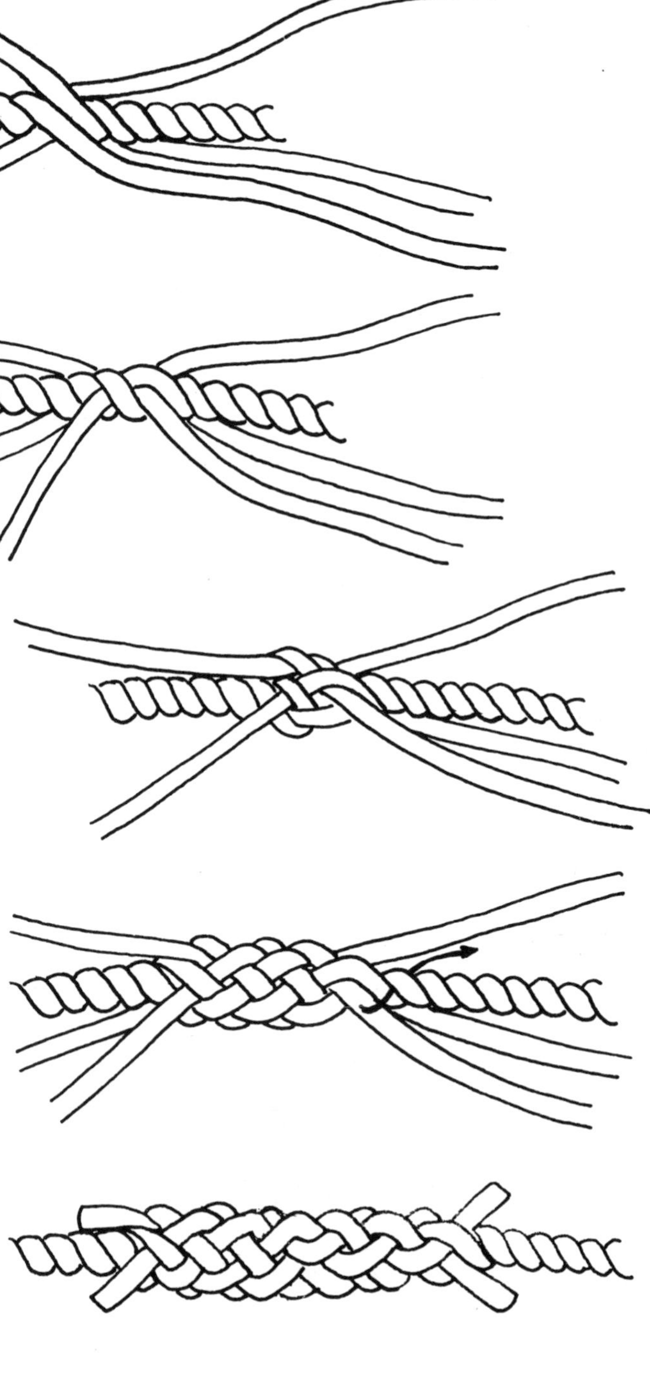

In the short splice, the end of each rope to be spliced is unlaid or untwisted for a short distance and the component cords of each rope are passed through the intact portion of the other. As each cord is passed or "tucked" through, it goes over one and under one of the coils of the intact rope in a spiral opposite in direction to the spiral of the coils of the intact rope (Diagram 94).

The short splice will always show regardless of how carefully it is done, because in the area of the splice, the diameter of the cord is increased.

The long splice is used to splice two ropes together without any abrupt bulge or increase in diameter of the cord. In this technique, a long length of rope is unlaid, about 15 times the diameter of the rope, and the two ends opposed as for the short splice. The cords however do not tuck through the other rope immediately, but spiral about it in the *same*

95. The long splice.

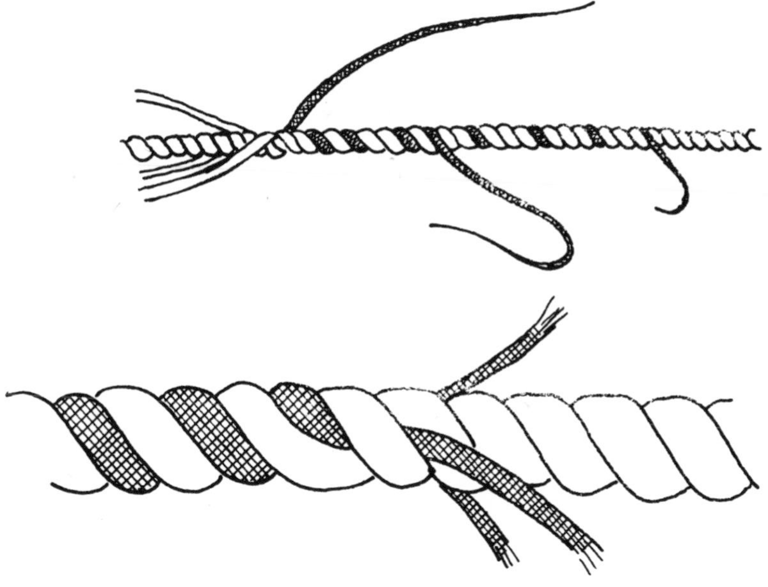

96. Variations of the short splice.
1. Side splice.
2. Eye splice.
3. Cut splice.
4. Back splice.

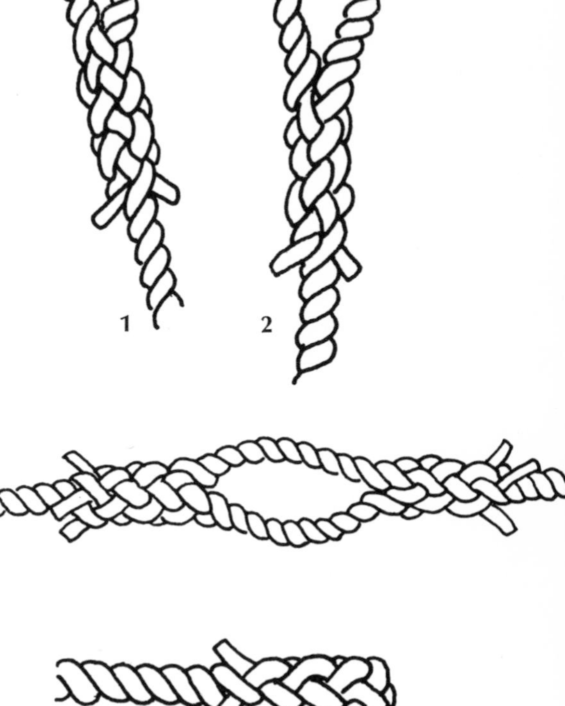

direction as the twist of the rope, lying in the groove between the coils of the rope, wedging them apart, so the new coil appears to match the existing coils. As the cords are spiraled about the rope, the threads in each cord are gradually thinned by cutting until the cord has decreased to about one third of its original diameter. Then the cords are tucked through the rope, but in the *same* direction as the spiral of the rope (see Diagram 95).

A splice holds because pull on the rope tends to tighten the spiral of its component cords so the tucked cords of the splice are clamped tighter. The greater the pull, the tighter the cords are held, up to the point at which the splice fails by separating.

Other splices such as the eye splice, cut splice, back splice, and side splice, refer to variations in the attachment of the ropes. The principle of the splicing remains the same (Diagram 96).

STOPPER KNOTS

Stopper knots form a knob or button on the end of a rope and are useful for ornamental finishing or for preventing a rope or cord from passing through a hole (Diagram 97). The simplest stopper knot is the man knot, a combination of the wall knot and the crown knot. Many other stopper knots are variations of the man knot or are similar to it and can be figured out from a sailor's knotting book once the man knot is mastered.

Most twisted cord used in macrame is 3 or 4 ply, that is, it has 3 or 4 component cords which were twisted together to make the larger cord or rope. We will show you how to do a man knot with 3 ply cord because the diagrams are simpler, but the principle is the same for cords or ropes of greater ply.

In a wall knot, the cords are unlaid and used to form loops, with each cord passing up and through the loop made by the adjacent cord passing in the direction of the twist of the rope. When the knot is complete, the cords of the rope point out and up from the end of the rope, as shown in Diagram 98.

97. Stopper knots prevent cord from slipping through a hole.

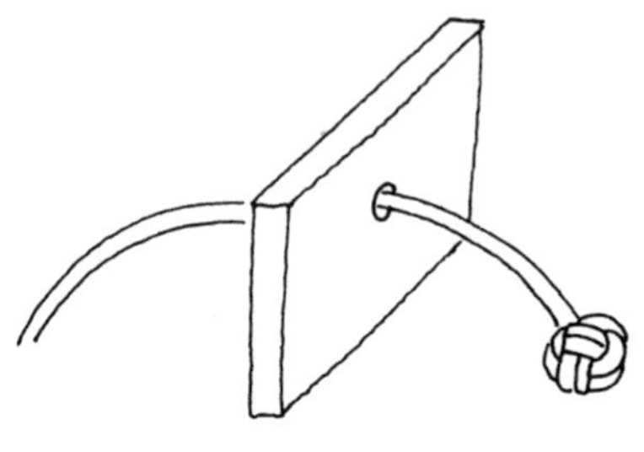

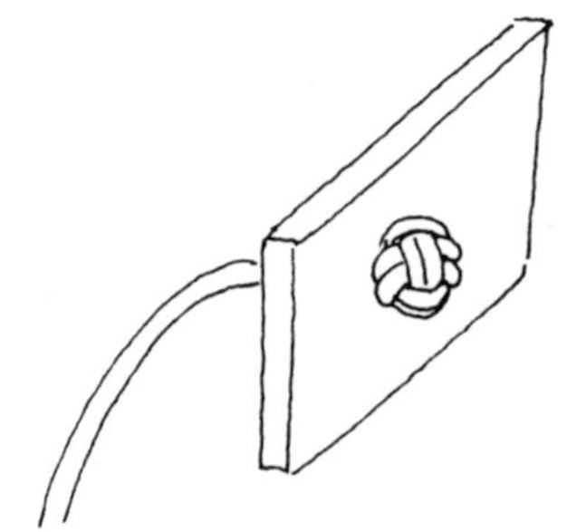

PHOTO SERIES E
The wall knot.

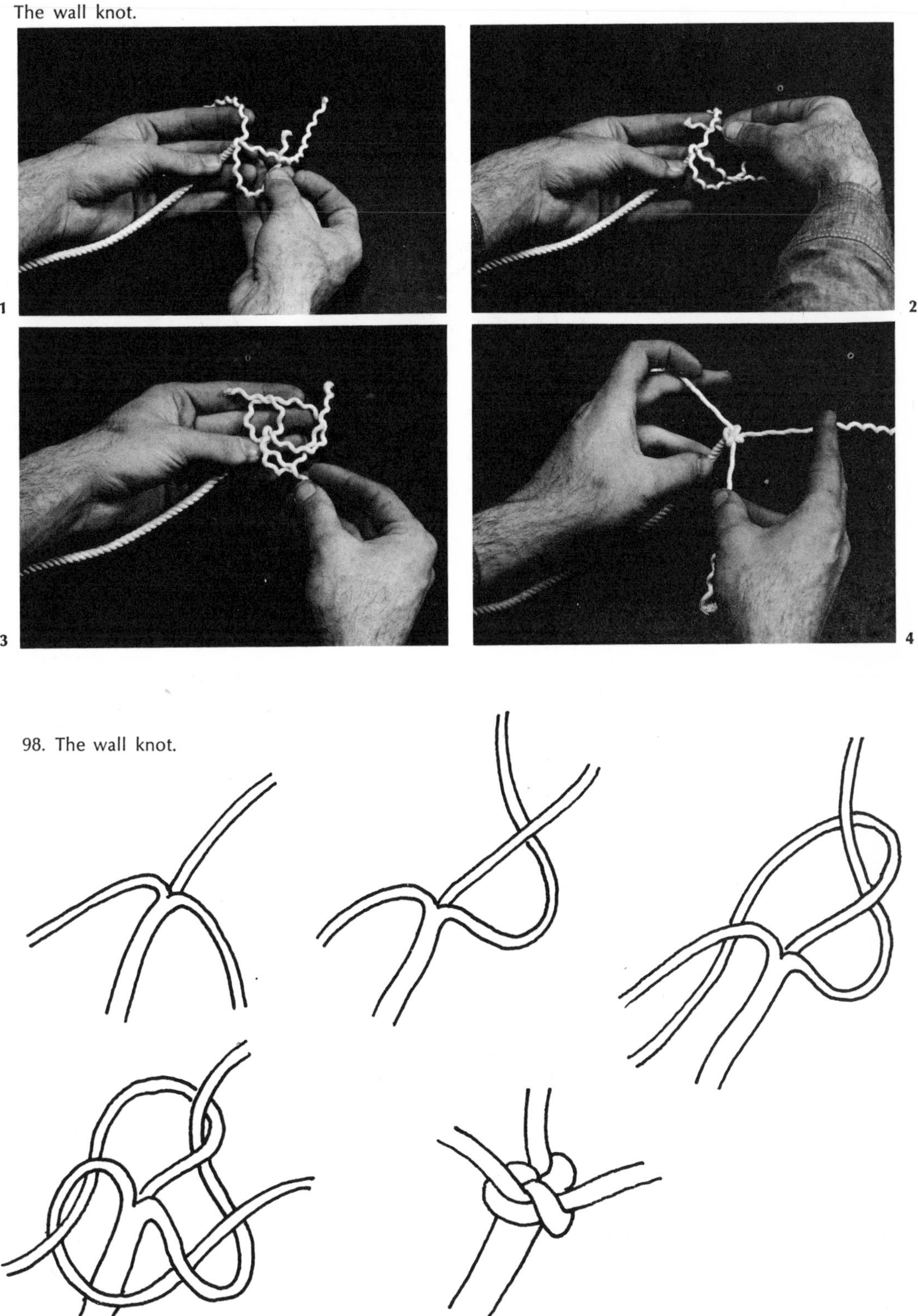

98. The wall knot.

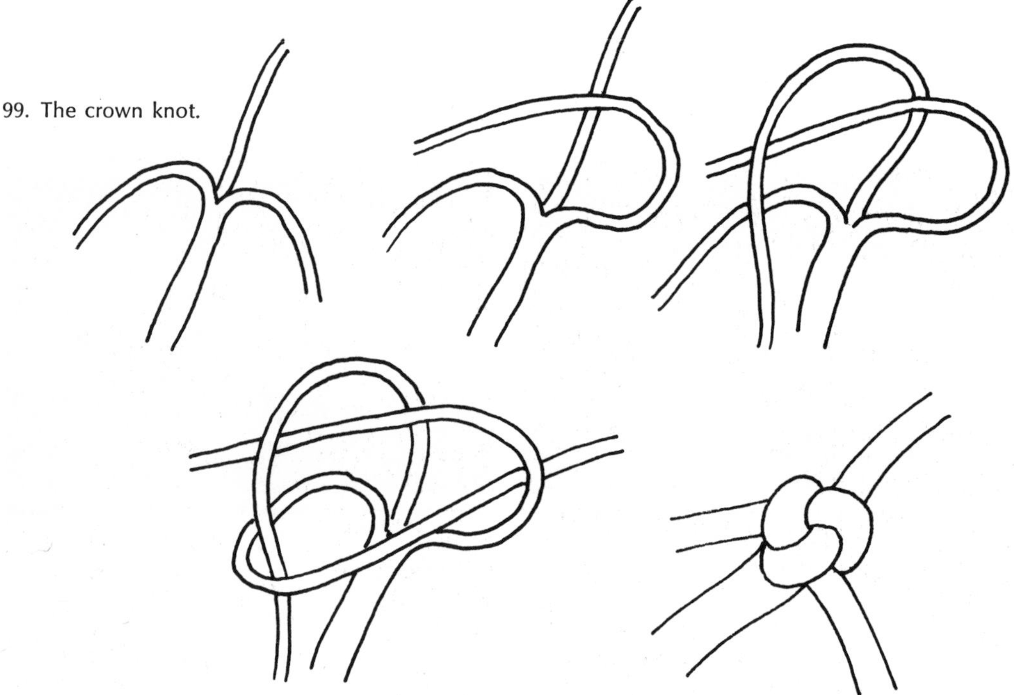

99. The crown knot.

100. The man knot—single, doubled, and tripled.

101. The crown knot used with the back splice.

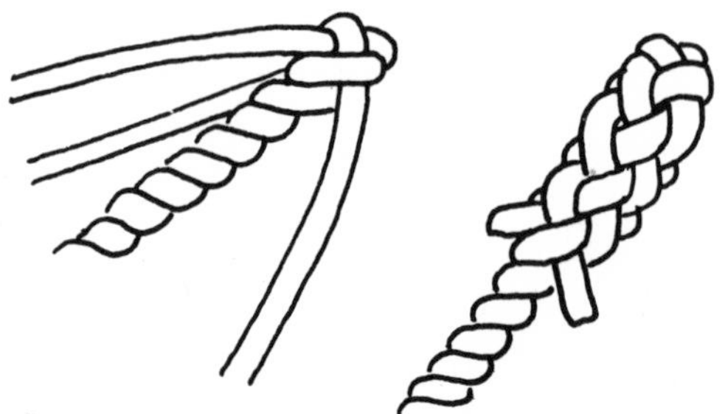

The crown knot is similar to the wall knot except the cords pass down and through the adjacent loops, so after the crown knot is tied, the cords point back toward the rope in the direction of its spiral (Diagram 99).

A wall knot topped by a crown knot, when doubled, is called a man knot. As with most stopper knots, this one is usually "doubled" or "tripled" to increase the size of the knob and enhance its appearance (Diagram 100). The knot is finished by passing the ends down through the center of the knot and trimming them short or working a backsplice with them.

Similar knots include the single and double Matthew Walker knots.

The crown knot by itself is useful whenever you want to reverse the direction of the cords at the end of a rope, as when starting a backsplice (Diagram 101).

Figures 40 and 41. Doubling the man knot with a hemostat.

40

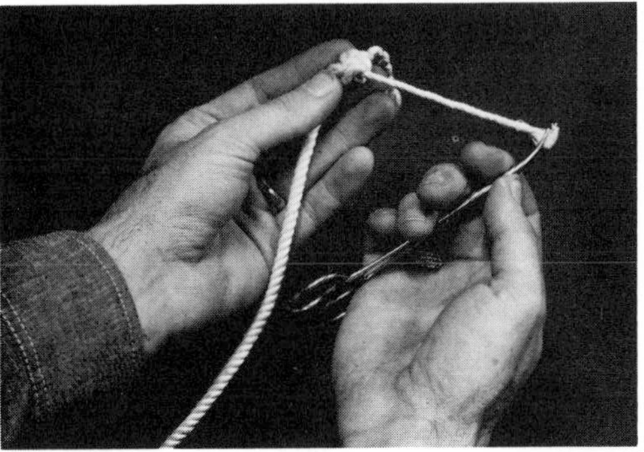

41

Figure 42. Man knots and backsplices used in a hanging planter.

BEADS AND LUMPS

Stopper knots can also be tied in the middle of a cord or rope, by untwisting half the line, tying the knot and retwisting the cords into rope again. This method works well with manila or hemp rope, but it is usually not possible to retwist cotton cord or rope properly, and it won't look the same as the intact part. If you want to tie a series of lumps or beads in the middle of cord, it's best to use another method. To create a length of cord with beads on it, you may use several means. Thin cord or thread may be sewn through and wrapped around a heavier cord or rope to form a "knot" on the line (see Diagram 102).

A turk's head tied in light cord also can be placed on rope or cord and tightened around the cord (Diagram 103). If the rope is first wrapped with thread or thin cord, the turk's head may be tied over the bulge created by the thread (Diagram 104).

A quick way to make a bead on a heavy cord is to twist the cord against the direction of its spiral until the component cords separate and spiral on their own beside the larger cord or rope (Diagram 105). If you twist the cord about 10 times and then pull firmly on it, the backward spirals you have created will be locked in and will stay without any further securing.

102.

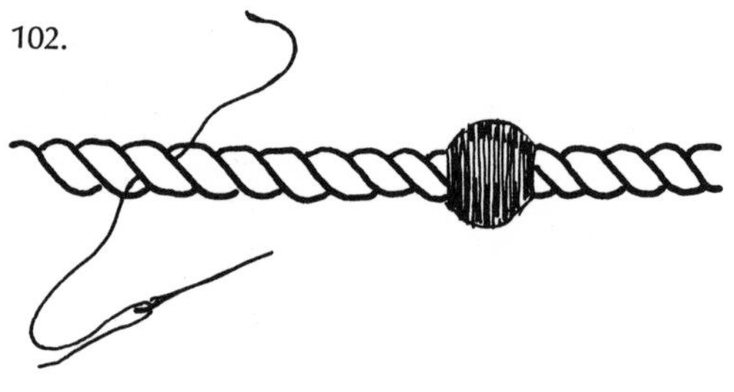

103.

104.

105. Twisting a cord against its spiral to make a decorative lump in the cord.

PHOTO SERIES F

Creating a "bead" in cord by twisting it against its natural spiral.

1

2

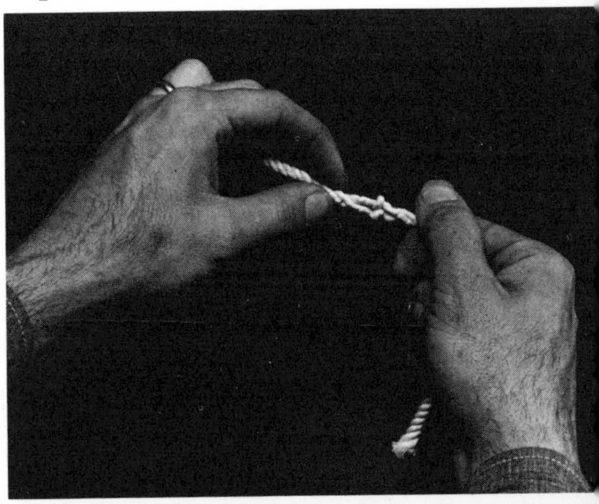

3

4

MAT KNOTS

Mat knots, or mats, are flat ornamental knots used for decoration rather than for working purposes. Hundreds of mat designs have been evolved by sailors, who are particularly fond of this style of decoration. The more complicated mats appear bewilderingly complex, but are based on the same principles as the simplest ones.

Mats, particularly large or complicated ones, are usually tied from a plan or diagram by working on a tying board with nails or brads to locate and stabilize key points in the design (see Diagram 106).

In most patterns, each cord of the finished mat will pass alternately over and under each cord it crosses. This weaving process gives the mat its stability and prevents collapse when the knot is removed from the tying board.

As with the turk's heads, mats are usually doubled or tripled for better appearance. The ends of the cords are glued or side spliced to finish, again as with the turk's heads.

There are many "families" of mats in which a basic pattern has been varied or combined to produce related more complex designs. To illustrate, the carrick bend (Josephine knot) gives rise to a simple circular mat when tied with a single cord, instead of two cords (Diagram 107).

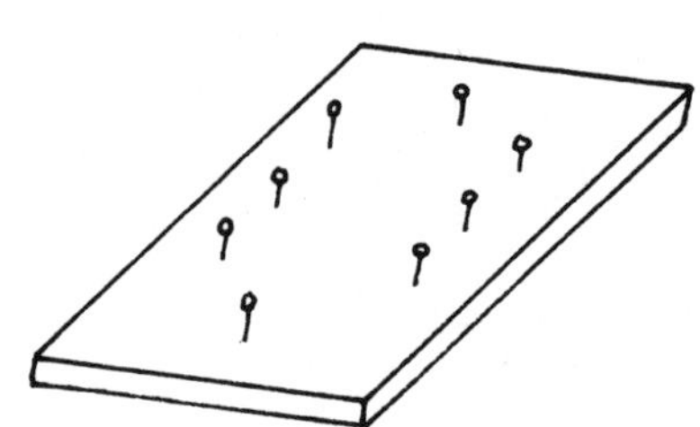

106. Tying jig for mat knots.

PHOTO SERIES G
Tying the carrick bend (Josephine knot).

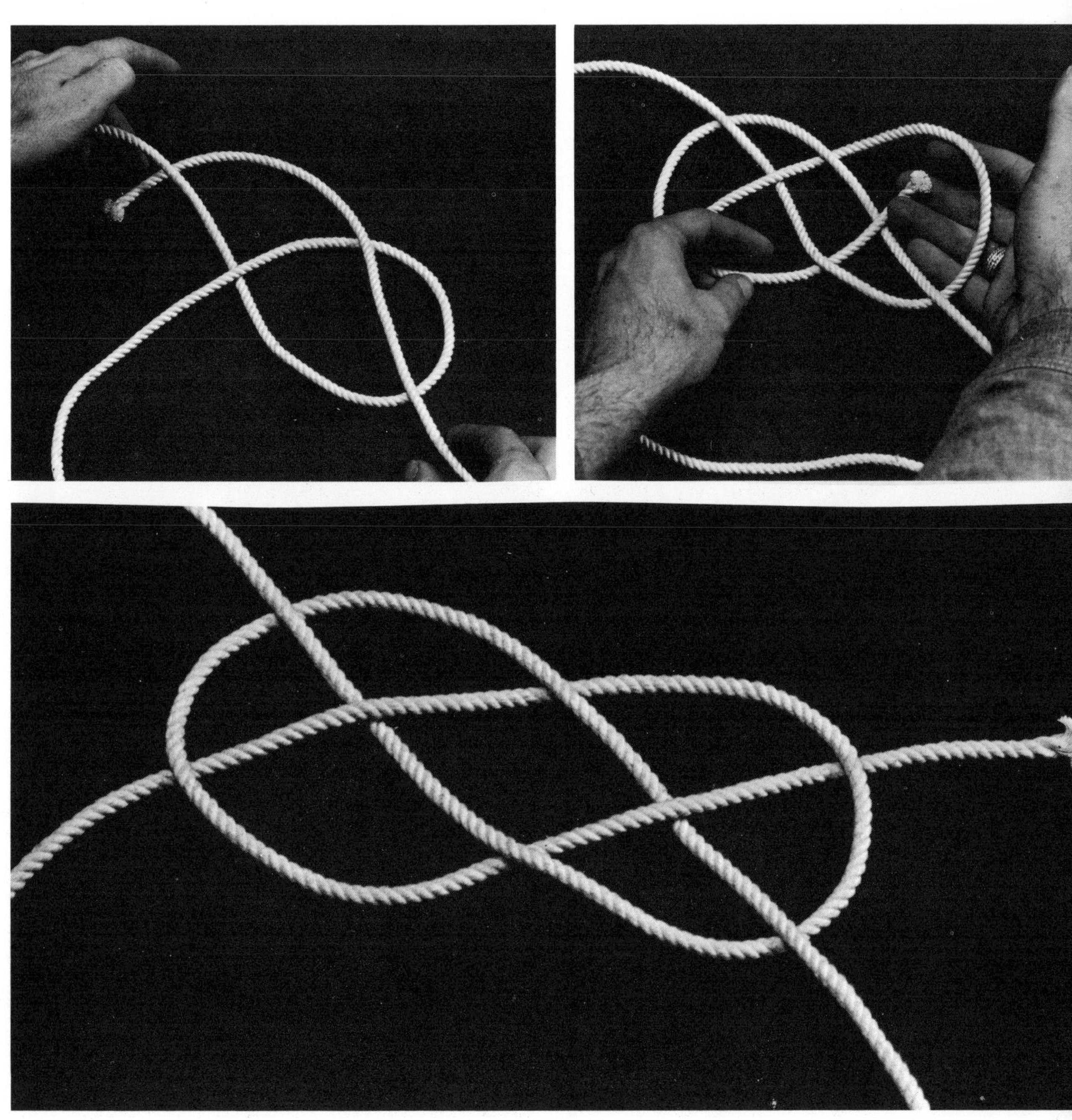

107. The carrick bend and the carrick bend mat.

PHOTO SERIES H
The round carrick bend mat, shown tied tripled with the ends finished by gluing and trimming the ends on the back.

1

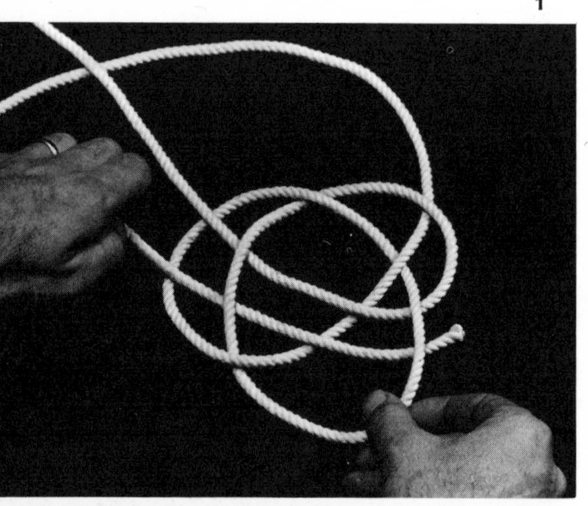

2

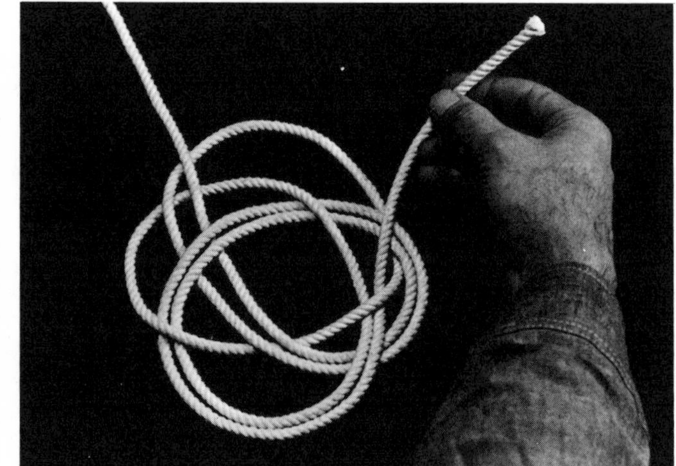

3

4

108. Figure-of-eight mats.

109. The star mat.

Carrick bends can also be continued to make the traditional figure-of-eight mats with two, three, four, or more parts. Diagram 108 shows figure-of-eight mats with 4 and 5 parts. The star mat in Diagram 109 is also a form of carrick bend mat in which the cords are led into each bend from the same side, rather than opposite sides as in the usual method of tying the knot. Star mats may be tied with two or more "points."

Figure 43. The start of a 4 part figure-of-eight knot or a 4 part star knot.

110. The "pretzel," which is the basis of the pretzel mats.

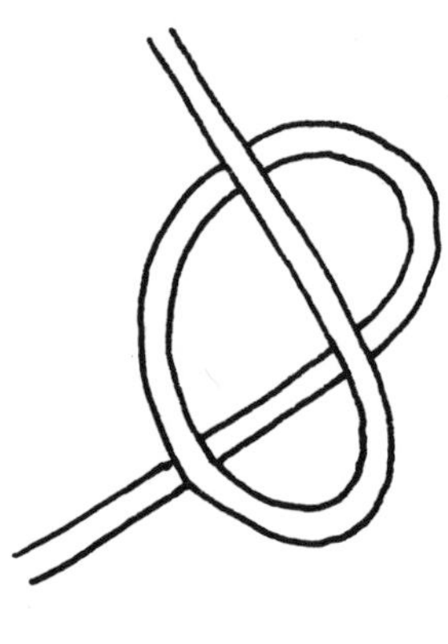

111. The ocean knot and the ocean mat.

"Pretzel mats" also comprise a family of knots in which the basic form is a pretzel-shaped loop of cord instead of the simple eight of a carrick bend (Diagram 110).

The ocean mat (Diagram 111) is a form of the pretzel mat equivalent to the round carrick bend mat, consisting basically of two superimposed pretzel shapes interwoven for stability. The basic pretzel shapes may also be combined as shown in Diagram 112, which depicts a mat similar to the figure-of-eight mats made from carrick bends. Like figure-of-eight mats, pretzel mats may be tied with more parts than the mat shown by adding more "pretzels."

Turk's head mats are simply turk's heads which have been opened up and laid flat. Diagram 113 shows the 3 part 4 turn turk's head as a mat. Diagram 114 shows the 3 part 10 turn and the 3 part 14 turn turk's head mats.

More complex turk's heads may also be made into mats, such as the 5 part 8 turn mat in Diagram 115.

112. Pretzel mats.

113. The simplest turk's head mat.

114. Turk's head mats (three part ten turn and three part fourteen turn).

115. The five part eight turn turk's head as a mat.

116 through 120. Representative mat knots.

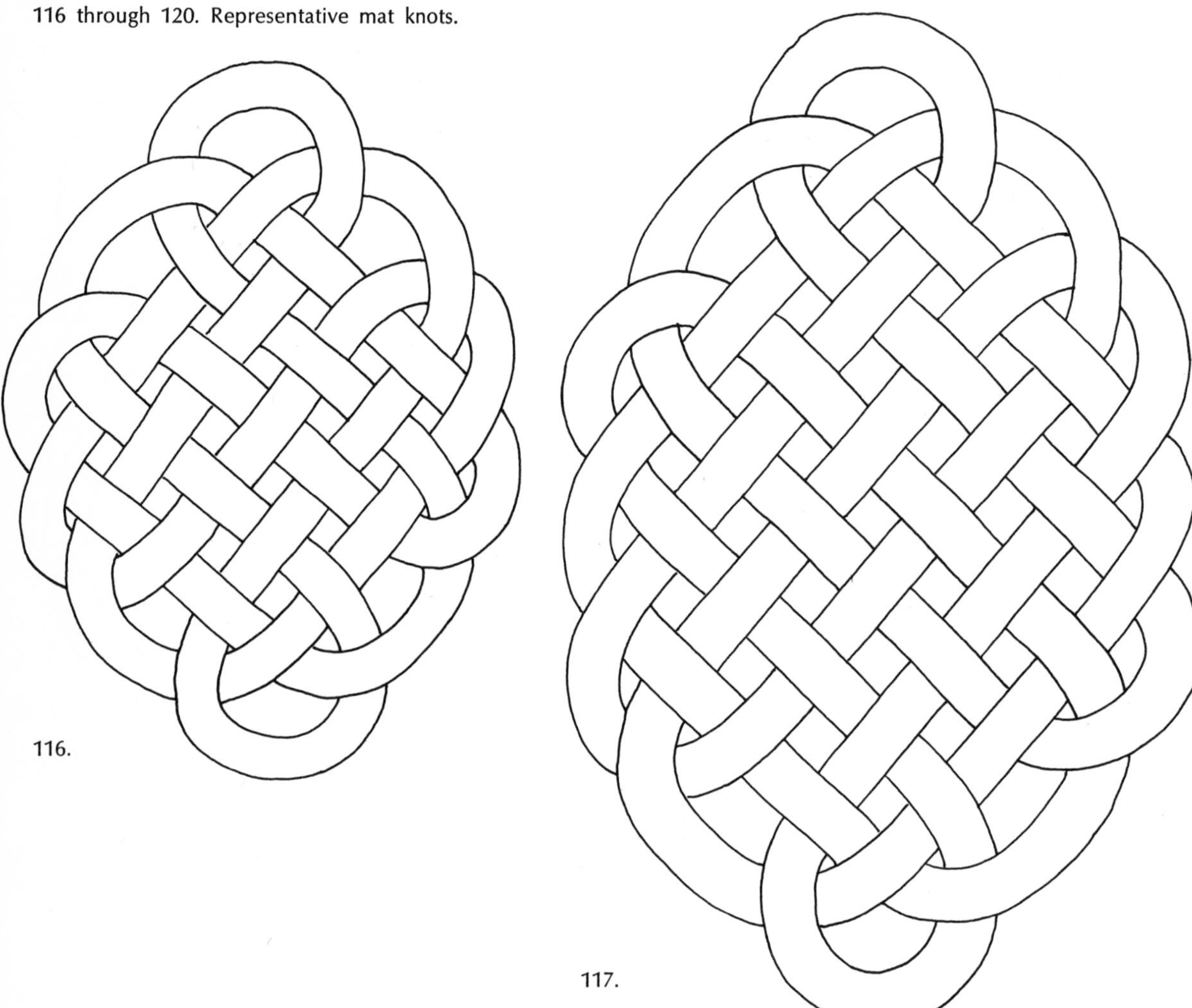

116.

117.

More complicated mats are usually variations of the simple mats just discussed and were developed by trial and error over the years. Many are traditional designs known by different names in different regions or different countries. Diagrams 116 to 120 show a few examples. Clifford Ashley's book and the *Encyclopedia of Knots* include many other patterns for those who are interested (see p. 158).

118.

119.

120.

121. Hanging bottles.

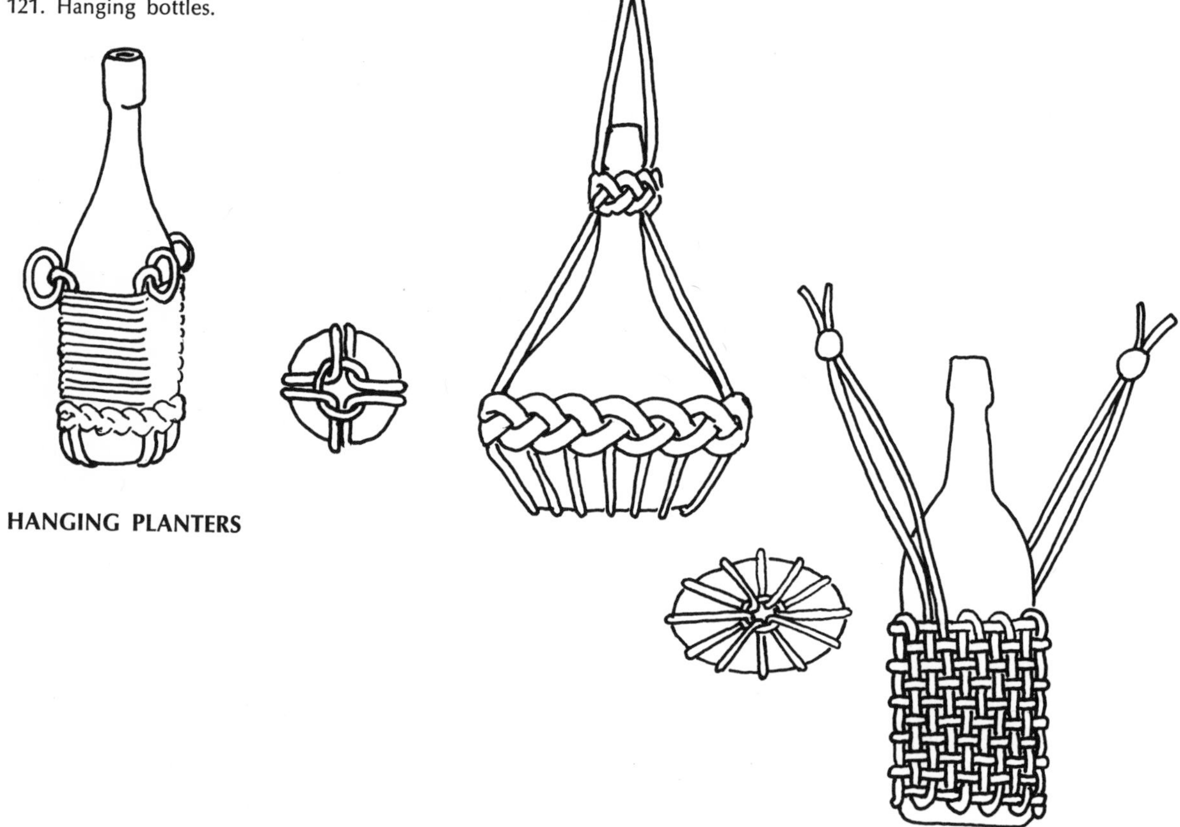

HANGING PLANTERS

Nearly any pot or planter can be suspended by cord or string if you know how to support it properly. One method involves tying a basket or cradle which supports the planter and is in turn suspended by the hanging cords. This method can be used for bottles, cans, or pottery containers of various shapes, as long as the planter is securely held and supported by the basket of cord.

For example, to suspend a wine bottle or crock, you should tie a basket which supports the weight of the bottle by passing under it, and which prevents the bottle from tipping, by passing around the neck of the bottle or around the body of the bottle about two thirds of the way up. This basket of cord is then supported by the cords used to suspend the bottle. Several examples are shown in Diagram 121.

Ceramic planters can be hung similarly (Diagram 122). Another type of hanging planter requires a pot specifically made for hanging. The simplest example is a pot with holes in the rim and is hung by heavy cord spliced together and tipped with stopper knots (Diagram 123).

Pots may have grooves or rings molded in them to facilitate hanging (Diagram 124).

Whatever design you use for hanging a planter, remember that the cord must withstand exposure to the elements, especially if it is used outside. Cotton cord will soon rot unless treated with varnish or preservative. Nylon, Dacron, or polypropylene should last indefinitely.

If you hang a pot by the rim, be sure that the rim is strong enough to support the weight of the pot, water, soil, and plant without breaking.

122. Hanging flowerpots.

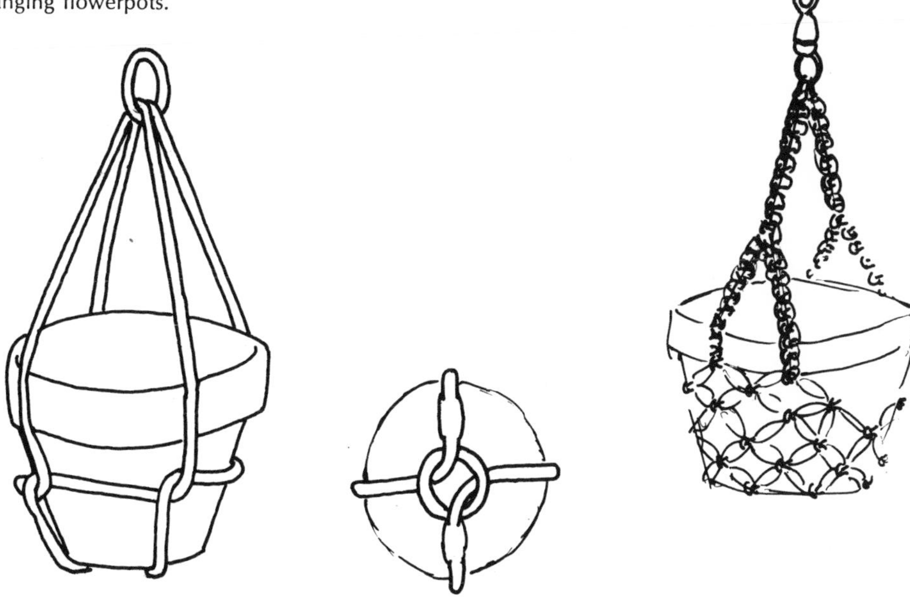

123 and 124. Pots made especially for hanging—see your local potter.

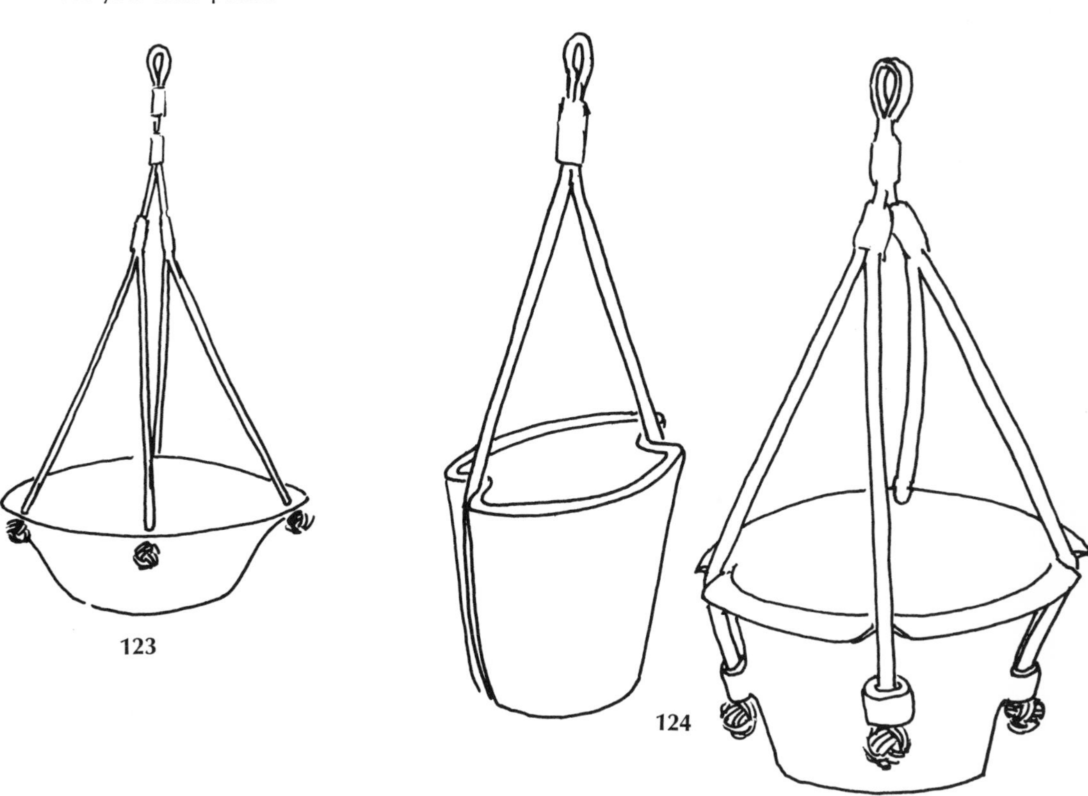

PRESERVING CORD

Untreated cord and yarn of most natural fibers are subject to decay. The rate and type of decay depends on the fiber and the conditions to which it is exposed.

Cotton and hemp-type fibers rot fairly rapidly when exposed to the elements. Extremes of temperature and humidity weaken and disrupt the fibers, and moisture makes a ground for the growth of the microorganisms causing rot. Insects and animals, too, can damage or destroy cord.

There are several ways to preserve cotton or hemp cord which will be used outside. In the old days, ships' rigging was tarred and wrapped with cloth strips. Various tar compounds and oil-base wood and rope preservatives are still available today. Most are effective against rot and insects, but may be dangerous to use. Creosote and similar compounds can cause severe eye injuries. Do not use any compound containing mineral spirits or distilled petroleum compounds on any cord to be handled by children. If it is safe to use this kind of preservative, you can choose from compounds which are clear or contain various stains. They are used as preservative treatments for wood siding and can be found at a lumberyard or building supply dealer.

Other less toxic preservatives include linseed oil, varnish, and various plastics. Varnish and plastic treatment will stiffen the cord and are therefore unsuitable for some pieces. Linseed oil won't stiffen the cord, but will weather away and the piece should be treated two or three times a season for adequate protection.

The best way to apply any liquid preservative except varnish or liquid plastic is to soak the piece in it. In brushing on varnish and plastic, be careful to work the material into the cord. Spray application of any varnish or plastic will accentuate the minute fibers protruding from cord or rope, whereas brushing will flatten these fibers and make the cord smoother in appearance.

Two to three coats of varnish will provide adequate protection for the cord; four to six coats will make the cord rigid and woodlike. Add stains and pigments to the varnish or plastic if you want to color the cord.

Another solution to the problem of cord preservation is the use of cord made of synthetic fibers resistant to decay. Nylon, Dacron, and polypropylene are widely used in cordage for marine use and there are many sizes and colors of cord and rope available today.

Nylon seine twine is good for outdoor use as it does not rot, but it chafes fairly easily.

Polypropylene and Dacron are also weather resistant and durable for outside use. None of the synthetic cords require special treatment for outdoor use.

GLOSSARY OF KNOTS

Knotting terminology is confused at best. Some names used currently are translations of French names; others are names used by lace-makers or hobbyists and are perplexing to the person adhering to sailors' usage.

In this section we use nautical terminology whenever possible, but we found wide variation among the reference texts we have consulted and in some cases have had to make an arbitrary decision.

Backsplice. See splice.

Bight. A simple loop of cord—not a knot.

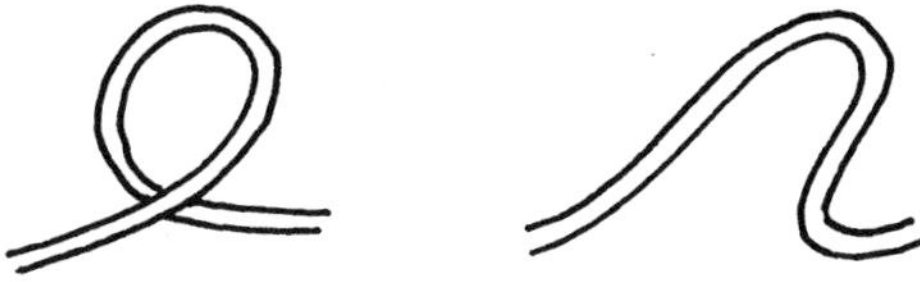

Blood knot. See overhand wrap knot.

Carrick bend (Josephine knot). A flat knot used to join two cords. See diagram 107

Clove hitch. A knot made with one cord by tying two half hitches as shown. Used to fasten a cord to some support. Diagram 57.

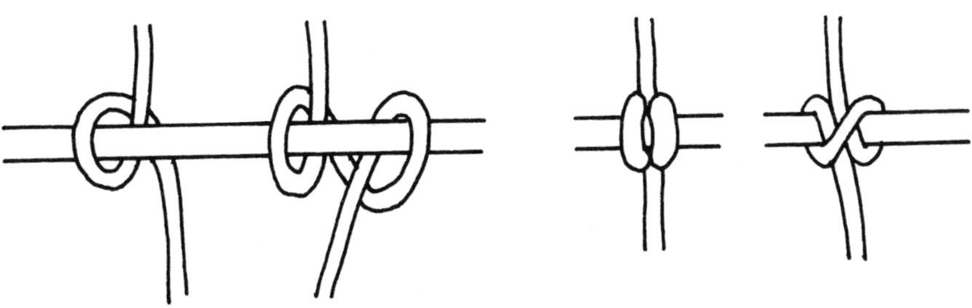

Crown knot. In splicing, the knot made by passing each cord of a rope down through a loop of the adjacent cord. *See* also man knot and Wall knot. Diagram 99.

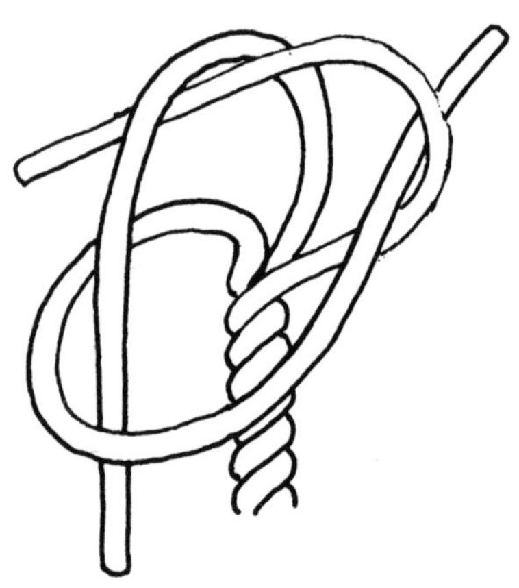

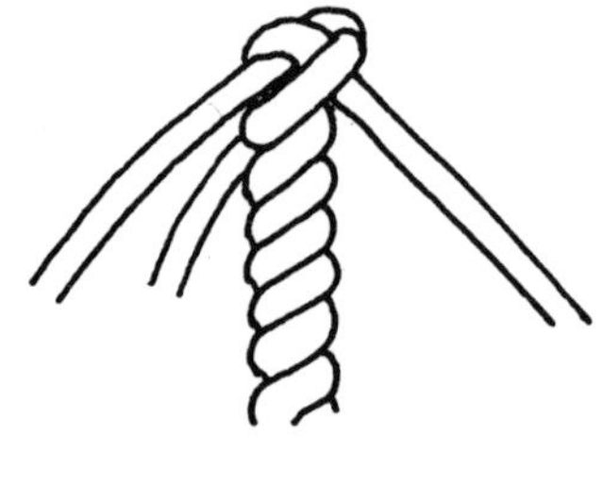

Eye splice. See splice.

Figure of eight knot. A knot tied with a single cord, often used as a stopper knot. Diagram 108.

Half hitch. Not a knot, just a loop of cord passing around a support. Two half hitches may be continued to form the clove hitch or the lark's head.

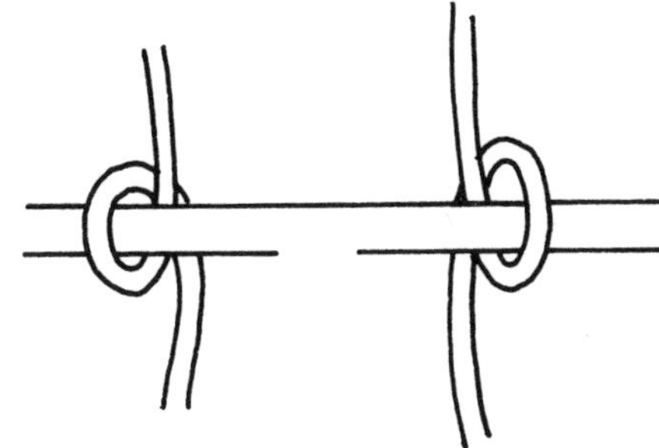

Hitching. General term for the nautical style of knotting in which some structure is completely covered by rope tied in patterns made up of combinations of half hitches.

Josephine knot. See carrick bend.

Lark's head. A knot tied with a single cord by tying two half hitches as shown. Used to fasten a cord to some support. Diagram 58.

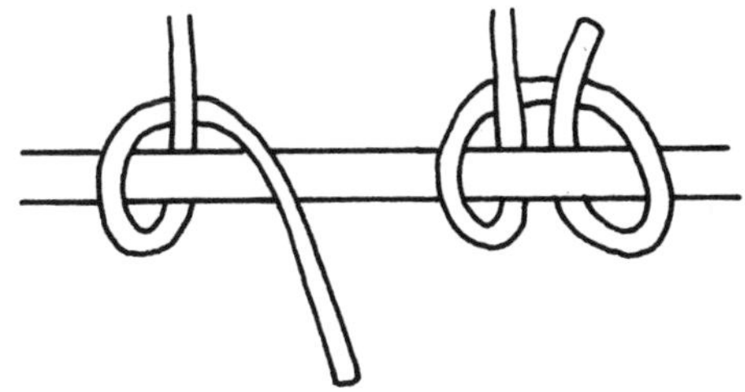

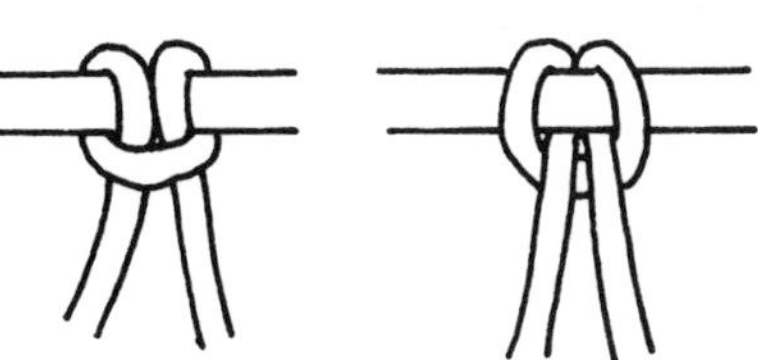

Long splice. See splice.
Macrame knot. See square knot.
Man knot. A simple stopper knot made by doubling a wall knot and crown knot tied on the end of a rope. Diagram 100.

Overhand knot. A simple knot tied with a single cord as shown in Diagram 41.

Overhand wrap knot (blood knot). A variation of the overhand knot in which the end of the cord is passed around and through the loop of the knot repeatedly to increase the size of the knot. Diagram 37.

Side splice. See splice.

Splice. The joining of two ropes by opening up their component cords and interweaving them with the intact portion of the other rope. Splices are named according to the way in which the cords are joined—backsplice, eye splice, long splice, side splice.

Square knot. A knot tied with two cords, as in Diagram 30. When tied over two supporting cords, it may be termed a macrame square knot or macrame knot. The square knot may be tied left-handed or right-handed.

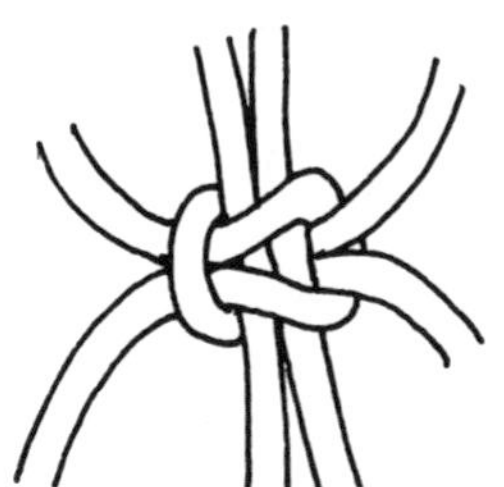

Stopper knot. General term for a knot used to make a lump on a cord for ornamental purposes, to prevent unraveling or to prevent the rope from running through a pulley.

Turk's head. Any one of a large series of knots which are closed circular braids made by passing a single cord repeatedly around in a circle with weaving steps to produce a stable knot.

Wall Knot. Stopper knot made by passing each cord of a rope through a loop of the adjacent cord. Diagram 98.

Bibliography: Books to Tickle Your Fancy

On Technique

The Ashley Book of Knots
Clifford W. Ashley
Doubleday & Co., N.Y., 1944.

Clear, systematic presentation of several thousand knots by a man in love with his subject.

Knots, Useful and Ornamental
George Russel Shaw
Bonanza Books, N.Y., 1934.

Nautical in orientation, with a good section on the Chinese and Japanese styles.

Encyclopedia of Knots and Fancy Rope Work
Raoul Graumont and John Hensel
Cornell Maritime Press
Cambridge, Md., 1970.

Thorough but sometimes cumbersome reference text.

Seventeenth-Century Rigging
Roger Charles Anderson
Percival Marshall & Co.
London, 1956.

How to do nearly anything with rope based on nautical techniques in the days before iron and steel rigging.

On Design

The Flowering of Art Nouveau
Maurice Rheims
Harry N. Abrams, Inc.
New York, 1966.

Documentation of a "movement" useful as a reference for design.

Gaudi
Lara Vinca Masini
Hamlyn, N.Y. 1969.

One man's vision of the world. Wow!

Arcology: The City in the Image of Man
Paolo Soleri
MIT Press, 1969.

Another man's vision.

List of Suppliers

LIST OF SUPPLIERS

Lily Mills Co.
Shelby, N. C. 28150

Frederick J. Fawcett, Inc.
129 S. Street, Boston, Mass. 02111

The Mannings
RD #2
East Berlin, Penna. 17316

The Makings
1916 University Ave.
Berkeley, Calif. 95704

House of Yarns
Route 1
Seabrook, N. H.

P. C. Herwig Co.
264 Clinton Street
Brooklyn, N.Y. 11201

The Sun Shop
7722 Maple Street
New Orleans, La. 70118

La Nasa Hardware Co.
1027 Decatur Street
New Orleans, La. 70116

Craft Yarns of Rhode Island
Box 385
Pawtucket, R. I. 02862

Index

Page numbers in italics indicate illustrations.